Sculpting Her Body Perfect

Brad Schoenfeld, CPT

**Personal Training Center for Women
Scarsdale, NY**

Human Kinetics

Library of Congress Cataloging-in-Publication Data

Schoenfeld, Brad, 1962-
    Sculpting her body perfect / by Brad Schoenfeld.
      p.   cm.
    ISBN 0-7360-0154-9
    1. Physical fitness for women.   2. Bodybuilding for women.
    I. Title.
    GV482.S37 1999
    646.7'5'082--dc21

                        99-25787
                          CIP

ISBN: 0-7360-0154-9

Acquisitions Editor: Martin Barnard; **Managing Editor:** Cynthia McEntire; **Assistant Editor:** Laurie Stokoe; **Copyeditor:** Robert R. Replinger; **Proofreader:** Sue Fetters; **Graphic Designer:** Nancy Rasmus; **Graphic Artist:** Francine Hamerski; **Photo Editor:** Clark Brooks; **Cover Designer:** Jack W. Davis; **Photographer (cover):** Terry Wild; **Photographer (interior):** Terry Wild, except where otherwise noted; **Medical Illustrator:** Kristin Mount; **Printer:** Versa Press

Human Kinetics books are available at special discounts for bulk purchase. Special editions or book excerpts can also be created to specification. For details, contact the Special Sales Manager at Human Kinetics.

Printed in the United States of America   10 9 8 7 6 5 4 3

Human Kinetics
Web site: www.humankinetics.com

United States: Human Kinetics, P.O. Box 5076, Champaign, IL 61825-5076
800-747-4457
e-mail: humank@hkusa.com

Canada: Human Kinetics, 475 Devonshire Road, Unit 100, Windsor, ON N8Y 2L5
800-465-7301 (in Canada only)
e-mail: hkcan@mnsi.net

Europe: Human Kinetics, P.O. Box IW14, Leeds LS16 6TR, United Kingdom
+44 (0) 113 278 1708
e-mail: humank@hkeurope.com

Australia: Human Kinetics, 57A Price Avenue, Lower Mitcham, South Australia 5062
08 8277 1555
e-mail: liahka@senet.com.au

New Zealand: Human Kinetics, P.O. Box 105-231, Auckland Central
09-309-1890
e-mail: hkp@ihug.co.nz

This book is dedicated to my brother, Glenn, who opened my eyes to the world of fitness. His guidance and encouragement inspired me to reach my personal best.

Contents

Foreword

Bodysculpting is both an art and a science.

The art of bodysculpting for women lies in creating a balanced, symmetrical physique that flows beautifully from one muscle to the next. You alone are the artist and can decide how you want the finished product—your body—to look. You can tone, reduce, enlarge, or shape any muscle that you choose. You can even accentuate certain muscles to hide genetic flaws, forming the illusion of wider shoulders or a smaller waist. Whatever direction you decide to take, you will be able to turn your body into a work of art.

The science of bodysculpting involves learning the fundamental principles and techniques of training. To become an artist, you must have a clear grasp of these facets and be able to implement them properly. Although you may have heard advertisements touting an easy way to a great physique, I can state unequivocally that there are no quick fixes. Without a sound training philosophy and a great deal of hard work, achieving the body of your dreams will be next to impossible.

Sculpting Her Body Perfect will teach you the science of bodysculpting so that you too can become an artist. It will provide you with all the tools you need to control your physical destiny. Everything is laid out in an easy-to-follow manner, guiding you on a step-by-step path to maximizing your body's potential. Exercise can be confusing to the novice trainee—this book makes it simple to understand.

Brad has provided a wealth of information, detailing an efficient, effective program that will help you achieve your ideal physique. His system is standardized so that any woman can implement it, yet it is flexible enough that you can adapt it to your individual genetic abilities and limitations. After you have mastered the concepts found in these pages, you will truly be an artist, with the power to shape your body almost any way you choose.

Although exercise will not provide instant gratification, you should begin to see results within a short time. Even though everyone's body responds slightly differently to working out, your progress will be fairly rapid if you maintain a dedicated fitness regimen. After only a month or so, you should start to notice changes in your overall shape and definition. Thereafter, gains should continue at a steady rate and, before long, you will see your body transform before your very eyes.

I am delighted that Brad has asked me to write the foreword for this book because I share many of the ideals it puts forth. I hope my endorsement of Brad's philosophy and methods can inspire you as to what you can accomplish by adhering to these ideals and leading a fitness lifestyle. By training consistently, eating healthy foods, and surrounding yourself with positive influences, a strong, shapely body can be yours. If you have the will to succeed, there is virtually no limit to what you can achieve. Embrace this book as your bodysculpting bible and I guarantee it will change the way you feel about your body—and yourself— forever!

Kiana Tom

Host and producer of
ESPN2's "Kiana's Flex Appeal"

High praise for Brad Schoenfeld's *Sculpting Her Body Perfect:*

"Wow! Seldom have I read such a comprehensive and well-researched source on women's fitness. Not only does the reader receive an excellent selection of optimum exercises for each body part, but the kinesiology and logic behind the selections is outstanding."

Lovenia Tuley

Ms. Fitness America finalist

"A clearly written book with a wealth of information for both beginners and advanced female exercise enthusiasts or personal trainers."

Shannon Meteraud

Miss Super Fitness

"Finally, an understandable training manual that will help a woman achieve her fitness goals. An outstanding guide that is not only interesting but effectively written by someone knowledgeable in the field!"

Rikki Rife

Fitness model

"The philosophy behind Brad's training system has enabled me to develop a figure that allows me to appear in the swimsuit editions of the top fitness magazines."

Tina Jo Bagne

Ms. Galaxy finalist

Acknowledgments

To Bob Silverstein for your diligence, patience, and sound advice in bringing this book to life. You're not only a great agent but a true friend.

To Martin Barnard and Cynthia McEntire for trimming the fat and sculpting this book to perfection. Your insight and ideas were invaluable.

To my parents for supporting me in my dream. You've always been there for me.

To all my clients, past and present, at the Personal Training Center for Women, who helped me perfect the High-Energy Fitness system and provided the impetus for this book.

To all the trainers, past and present, who have worked at the Personal Training Center for Women, who helped me impart the High-Energy Fitness system to a legion of women.

To Suzanne Robbins for helping me hone my writing skills.

To Amy Tutera, Clarissa Chueire, Anastasia Schepis, Linda Giulanti, Jackie Roberts, Michelle Gabriele, Cindy Goldmintz, and Jane Imburgia for making the photo shoot run so smoothly. Your professionalism was greatly appreciated.

To Gina Mazzarella for having a special impact on my life. Forever and always.

To Joe Weider for helping to bring fitness into the mainstream and expanding my knowledge in the early years.

To Kiana Tom, Debbie Kruck, Laurie Donnelly, Carol Semple-Marzetta, Donna Richardson, Lovenia Tuley, Michelle Ralabate, Lori Ann Lloyd, Shannon Meteraud, Rikki Rife, Tina Jo Bagne, Karen Hulse, Michelle Bellini, and all the other great fitness models that have embraced the High-Energy Fitness system and lent support. Your endorsements have validated my life's work.

A special thanks to Gold's Gym in White Plains, NY, for use of their fine fitness facility in the photo shoot. You guys are the best!

Introduction

You are about to set out on a journey to physique heaven—a place where you have achieved your ideal physique. The long, winding road that leads to this paradise is not an easy one to travel. But with dedication, persistence, and patience, as well as much hard work and sweat, you can complete the journey.

The human body is one of the most complex mechanisms in the world. No invention—computer, machine, or any other device—can approach the intricacy of the human body. The body chemistry of a woman is especially complex compared to a man's. Women have many physical and mental challenges that convolute the training process—issues not pertinent to men.

Creating a productive exercise regimen is thus a daunting task. Although some gender differences are obvious, more subtle variances can profoundly affect exercise capabilities. Let's discuss some of the physiological and psychological dilemmas that make women's fitness such an involved enterprise.

• *Women possess significantly less muscle than men*. The average man has about twice the muscle mass as the average woman. Because women do not develop considerable muscular bulk, achieving a hard body is significantly more difficult. Muscle tissue can be shaped and refined (as opposed to fat, which cannot), and the less muscle there is to shape, the more difficult it is to promote muscle tone. Decreased muscle mass also abates resting metabolic rate, adding to the disadvantage women have in attempting to improve muscular definition.

• *Women produce substantially less testosterone than men*. Testosterone is a hormone that produces male characteristics such as facial hair, deepening of the voice, and so forth. For a woman, testosterone is a double-edged sword. On the one hand, women secrete only a limited amount of testosterone and thus are able to maintain feminine features. Excessive testosterone production would give a woman masculine traits—an unwelcome prospect for most women. On the other hand, testosterone happens to be one of the primary factors in promoting muscular development. Hence, decreased testosterone production makes it difficult to improve the quality of one's muscle. You cannot shape what you do not have and, with limited testosterone production, it is a struggle to accrue appreciable muscle tone.

• *Women have a greater amount of body-fat stores than men.* Obviously, the accumulation of fat will obscure muscle tone. The more fat a person stores, the less likely it is that muscle tone will be apparent. Making matters worse, women tend to develop cellulite—fat deposited in clumps in specific areas of the body. This is often genetic, and can sometimes remain even when body fat is relatively low. To counteract these influences, strict attention to nutrition and training is mandatory.

• *The menstrual cycle creates a hormonal fluctuation that can disrupt a woman's state of well-being.* Many women develop cramps, nausea, and fatigue in conjunction with their menstruation, sometimes accompanied by feelings of irritability and depression. These symptoms can make training difficult. Compounding this problem, significant fluid retention and cravings for sweets frequently accompany the premenstrual period. This can often induce temporary weight gain and edema, further impeding a woman's impetus to train.

• *Women generally have decreased bone density compared with men.* As a rule, women tend to have delicate bone structures. This makes them particularly prone to conditions such as osteoporosis. Because the skeletal structure assists the muscles in exercise performance, reduced bone density can hamper training. Often, a woman's joints will be weaker than her muscle, causing her to abort an exercise before she fully stimulates the target muscle. Additionally, accompanying joint pain will frequently develop due to structural frailty. This is especially true in the wrists and elbows, making the performance of certain exercises troublesome.

• *Pregnancy will often change a woman's hormonal balance and can alter her physiologic structure.* When a woman goes through pregnancy, major biological changes take place within her body. Certain areas will expand, others will stretch, and still others will sag due to the demands of childbearing. Metabolism often slows down dramatically during this period, and excessive food cravings will often cause a woman to gain an inordinate amount of weight. Many of these things will carry over into the postpartum period (including the effects from any surgery) and can greatly alter a woman's fitness abilities.

• *Women tend to be self-conscious about their bodies.* In general, men are comfortable with their physiques. A guy can look in the mirror and believe that by losing a few pounds, he could be the next Mr. America. Women, on the other hand, are more insecure about their bodies. They generally see themselves as being fat and out of shape—regardless of their actual proportions. One characteristic of anorexic women is that they are obsessed with being overweight (although they might be five feet, five inches tall and weigh only 90 pounds!). This often leads to a preoccupation with training and consequently causes an overtrained state (the detriments of which will be discussed later in this book).

• *Women are frequently intimidated by hard physical labor and strength-related activities.* Women are often taught from a young age that strenuous activities are not meant for them. Physical labor is not considered feminine in our culture, and the belief that large muscles are required to carry out these tasks furthers this line of thinking. It is common for a woman to ask a man to perform chores like lifting packages or moving objects, although she could do it herself. This mentality can cause an aversion to undertaking a strenuous exercise regimen.

These factors, among others, complicate a woman's ability to optimize her physique. You might think that with all this working against you, achieving results would be almost impossible. I can assure you that this is not the case. A dedicated fitness regimen is practically guaranteed to generate results if you take the proper approach. I have trained women in their 40s, 50s, 60s, and even 70s who have made excellent progress. By following the system described, so can you.

I like to use the analogy that you should approach bodysculpting as if you were building a house. A builder constructing a house must first lay down a foundation. The foundation is what the house will rest on; without a solid foundation, the house will crumble. Next, the builder must erect a frame. The frame is built on the foundation and will support the floors and walls of the house. After the builder adds the walls and roof, the structure will begin to look complete. Finally, the builder can add the details of the house, such as marble tiles and mirrored walls, which give the house a finished look. The homeowner, at her discretion, can now make further improvements on an ongoing basis.

Similarly, in sculpting your body, you first must develop a foundation of muscle (body-conditioning phase). You need this foundation to have a base on which to work. This will also increase the solidity of your connective tissue and the strength of your joints, which are necessary in the performance of many advanced exercises. Next, you can begin the bodysculpting procedure by refining your muscle (toning and shaping phase). Your body will now start to take form, and your lines and curves will be accentuated with pleasing shape and symmetry. Last, you can fine-tune your physique by concentrating on details such as adding enhanced shape to your biceps or achieving more tone to your inner thighs (targeted bodysculpting phase). This is where bodysculpting becomes an art!

Considering the intricacies of women's fitness, you may wonder whether you should work out in a health club or perform this routine at home. Certainly, you do not *need* to go to a health club to enjoy the benefits of the High-Energy Fitness system. The program is adaptable to almost any training environment. For the best results, however, I highly recommend choosing a facility that has an array of fitness equipment. Just as a builder uses a variety of tools to erect a house, you can benefit from using a diversity of fitness devices to sculpt your body. Although it may be possible for a builder to construct a house using only a hammer and saw, it obviously would be a burdensome task. The end product would be compromised, and the project would take a great deal more time than it would if the builder had available a full complement of power tools. Similarly, if your access to fitness equipment is restricted, the possibilities for your routine will be limited. Inevitably, this will delay or restrain your progress.

Because you will be incorporating many exercises into your training routine, it is essential that you have a clear understanding of the form and function of various exercises. You must obtain basic motor skills before you can concentrate on the all-important principles of training. After you have acquired an appreciation of exercise function, you will be able to focus on these principles and apply them productively to facilitate results. Accordingly, you should study the exercise demonstrations in this book and commit these movements to memory so they become part of your subconscious.

Furthermore, throughout this book, I reference various anatomical and physiological principles. If you are not familiar with any of the terminology, please refer to the glossary for further explanation. Although I will strive to maintain a user-friendly approach, it is necessary to include some technical information. By making an effort to comprehend these terms, you will enhance your overall understanding of fitness.

The subject of fitness might seem overwhelming at this point. Perhaps you are wondering if this is really for you. It is often hard to see the big picture when you first undertake a fitness regimen and, to many women, the prospect of becoming disciplined with exercise is incomprehensible. This is especially true in the beginning phase of training, when the mind and body are not in tune with the stress of a fitness regimen. During this initial period, you must be patient and set realistic expectations for progress. Studies have shown that 80 percent of women who start an exercise program quit within the first 60 days. Usually this is caused by frustration from a lack of results. The majority of these women, however, begin the training process with virtually no strategy or plan of action. They have a poor comprehension of fitness and little idea how to generate results. Their chances of success are slim.

The High-Energy Fitness system will give you all the resources you need to enjoy success in the fitness arena. If you follow this system as outlined, you *will* achieve your goals. Be aware, though, that High-Energy Fitness is not an easy solution or a shortcut to physique heaven. On the contrary, it requires a great deal of hard work and disciplined effort to achieve desired results. With that in mind, you should be able to progress at a rapid, steady rate. In most cases, you should expect to notice visible changes in your body a month after undertaking the High-Energy Fitness system. Those who have the patience and motivation to persist will reap the many rewards associated with fitness, including enhanced strength, improved posture, elevated energy levels, increased bone density, reduced stress, and, of course, a terrific body!

Remember, you are in control of your efforts and should train at your own pace. Although following this program to its fullest extent will generate the best results, you can make impressive gains by using the program on a modified basis. As long as you adhere to the basic principles behind the High-Energy Fitness system, you can alter the scope of your routine as you see fit. Not everyone is willing or able to take High-Energy Fitness to its most advanced levels. Often it is not necessary to do so. Depending on your vision of the ideal female physique, you may be satisfied with the results from the basic body-conditioning routine. Whatever you desire, it is useful to maintain perspective about your ultimate fitness goals and proceed accordingly.

Finally, let the mirror be the ultimate gauge of your progress. Some women become obsessed with the scale and panic if they gain even a pound. Using the scale as a barometer, however, can be deceiving and counterproductive. For instance, the scale does not measure your body-fat percentage or water retention and thus can give a false reading of actual results. Muscle is much denser than fat and consequently will weigh more by volume. A golf ball, for example, can weigh more than a tennis ball even though it is much smaller. Similarly, with a proper fitness regimen, you can significantly decrease your body-fat percentage while actually adding weight. In this way, you redistribute your weight and can reduce your proportions by several dress sizes. Ultimately, weight is just a number that means little in the overall scheme of things. It is much more important to be happy with your shape and the way your clothes fit your body. In the end, let the way you look and feel be your guide to success.

1 Sculpting the Ultimate Body

Before applying the principles of High-Energy Fitness and beginning your routine, familiarize yourself with the supporting concepts and techniques to facilitate implementation of this program. Let's review some of the issues that will expedite your bodysculpting.

Know Your Muscles

Before setting out on your training odyssey, you should cultivate a working knowledge of anatomical musculature, especially the major muscles of your body. A common response to this statement is "Why do I need to know this? I don't care about the names or locations of my muscles. Just tell me what to do and let's start working out." This short-sighted approach, however, will eventually set back your long-term progress. Taking the time to learn the muscles of your body will help you immensely in shaping your physique and avoiding common training mistakes. The following are some of the benefits of acquiring knowledge of muscular anatomy:

• *It will help you visualize each muscle during training.* Your mind-to-muscle link is enhanced when you are able to create a mental image of the muscle that you are working. Developing a mind-to-muscle link allows you to isolate your muscles more effectively during training and direct stress away from undesired secondary muscle movers. Without a comprehension of muscular anatomy, you will find it

Mind-to-Muscle Link

The mind-to-muscle link is invaluable to the training process. Having a mind-to-muscle link means that you can visualize a muscle and feel it working through the range of motion of the exercise you are performing. This is a foreign concept to many, and its relevance to training might not be initially apparent. But until you develop a mind-to-muscle link, the effectiveness of your training will be severely limited.

Weight training is not merely the action of lifting a weight from point A to point B; it involves working a muscle through a range of motion. You can perform an exercise in what appears to be satisfactory form but fail to stimulate the target muscle adequately. For example, most beginning trainees think that a lat pulldown is an exercise for the biceps and forearms. Because the biceps and forearms initiate the movement of weight, the arms will necessarily receive stress during exercise performance. Without understanding the mind-to-muscle link, the trainee will be inclined to feel the movement in her arms. This will compel the trainee to use primarily her arms, rather than the target muscles of the upper back, to lift the weight. Doing so compromises the effectiveness of the exercise.

To induce maximal muscular stress, you must consciously visualize the muscle you are training and use that muscle exclusively to raise and lower the weight. Throughout each repetition, keep the target muscle under continuous tension, making sure to squeeze the muscle on the contraction. In the example of the lat pulldown, you must pull the weight down with the muscles of the upper back and then squeeze the scapula together when you reach the contraction phase of the movement. As you let the weight ascend, your back muscles should resist its gravitational force. Finally, when you approach the starting point of the exercise, you should feel a complete stretch in the lats, and, without hesitation, continue to the next repetition. By employing a mind-to-muscle link, you will channel the majority of stress to the target muscles of the upper back.

difficult to develop a satisfactory mind-to-muscle link and will subsequently fall short of maximizing your potential.

- *It will help improve your form in exercise performance.* Once you have a cognizance of muscular anatomy, the form and function of various exercises will be solidified in your mind. Because you are better able to understand the physics behind weight training, you can apply this knowledge to the biomechanics of exercise performance. This will help you notice inconsistencies in your form simply by understanding the path that a weight must travel to target a specific muscle.

- *It will help improve muscular control.* When you perform a set, the ability to maintain control over your muscles helps you get more out of each repetition. It is easier to exert more force into your contractions, increasing the intensity of your repetitions. Because muscular intensity is one of the primary factors in improving definition, it follows that you will improve your results by developing muscular control. This becomes even more important when using advanced training techniques.

- *It will help improve your ability to assess your physique.* Having knowledge of muscular anatomy will allow you to get more in tune

with your body. You will begin to notice your muscles (and those of others!) and understand how each muscle affects your overall proportions. This will enable you to assess your physique and know which muscles you need to train to sculpt your body in a shapely, feminine manner.

Although you now realize that it is advantageous to acquire a comprehension of muscular anatomy, learning the various muscles is a chore. The human body contains hundreds of muscles. Virtually every part of you—including your face, neck, torso, legs, and feet—has muscular components. Although learning about all of them is an imposing proposition, at this point you need only develop a basic awareness of your musculature.

Most relevant are the so-called "show muscles" of the body. These are the muscle groups that can alter the shape of your physique and help to produce aesthetic proportions. The fitness community generally recognizes nine major categories of show muscles. These major categories are essentially groups of muscles that encompass many individual muscles. For instance, the back is one of the major muscle groups. If you look at the back, you will see that it is composed of many muscles, including the latissimus dorsi, rhomboids, teres major, trapezius, and spinal erectors, among others. The individual muscles are essentially subcategories within the major muscle groups.

Table 1.1 shows each major muscle category and the individual muscles that make up the corresponding subcategories. I have listed the muscles that are of the greatest consequence in bodysculpting—the ones that will have the most impact on accentuating your proportions. To keep it simple, I have neglected to mention many of the smaller muscles in the body. These smaller muscles tend to be secondary muscle movers that act as stabilizers to the primary muscles. They will receive both direct and indirect stimuli during exercise performance, helping to contribute to their development. Unless you are aiming for a physique competition, these muscles will be of little consequence to your aesthetic proportions and you will not need to target them on an isolated basis.

A complete comprehension of the major muscle groups of your body is essential to your understanding of the theory behind the High-Energy Fitness system. Because your body contains only nine categories of major muscle groups, this should not be too difficult.

On the other hand, learning the individual muscles of the body is a more involved responsibility. If you do not have a background in science, the names (which are derived from ancient Latin and Greek) are difficult to pronounce, much less perceive. Do not worry, however, about specific muscular terminology or about remembering each muscle. For bodysculpting purposes, many of these names are shortened anyway—for example, the latissimus dorsi are the lats, the

Table 1.1   The Major Muscle Groups

Major muscle group	Individual muscles
Back	Teres major, latissimus dorsi, rhomboids, trapezius, erector spinae
Chest	Pectoralis major, pectoralis minor
Shoulders	Anterior deltoid, medial deltoid, posterior deltoid
Biceps	Biceps brachii, brachialis
Triceps	Triceps brachii
Quadriceps	Rectus femoris, vastus lateralis, vastus medialis
Hamstrings and glutes	Semitendinosus, semimembranosus, biceps femoris, gluteus maximus
Calves	Gastrocnemius, soleus
Abdominals	Rectus abdominis, obliques, serratus

rectus abdominis are the abs, and so on. Rather, you should develop an understanding of how they relate to each major muscle group and become aware of their approximate position on your body.

Pages 6 and 7 provide anatomical diagrams that delineate the location of these muscles. You can use these diagrams as a reference when a specific muscle is discussed. At this point, cultivate a general awareness of these muscles and make an effort to visualize the shape they take once they are developed. For instance, the triceps brachii (shortened to the tri's in bodysculpting lingo) is a three-headed muscle that sits on the back of the arm below the biceps (an area where many women tend to get flabby as the years go on). When properly developed, the triceps resemble a horseshoe and give the upper arms a tight, toned appearance. Visualizing the triceps in this fashion will reinforce your mind-to-muscle link and help you to actualize your ideal physique.

Compound and Isolation Movements

It is also important for you to be able to differentiate between compound and isolation movements—the two basic types of exercises used in weight training. The distinct characteristics of these movements provide unique options for bodysculpting. A well-structured routine will blend the movements to achieve maximum effect. As you become more experienced with weight training, optimally combining compound and isolation will be of critical consequence in shaping your physique.

As a rule, a compound movement will involve the action of two or more joints, while an isolation movement will involve only one joint. Consequently, many supporting muscles are involved in the completion of a compound movement. Certain compound movements, like the Olympic deadlift, require that you use virtually all the major muscles of the body. Isolation movements tend to target a specific muscle or muscle group, at the exclusion of secondary muscles. Because you use only one joint to lift a weight, rarely will supporting muscles come into play during exercise performance.

For example, the squat is a compound movement because it uses both the knee and hip joints to complete a repetition. As you descend into a squat position, both your knees and hips will bend to allow your body to move downward. Conversely, a leg extension is an isolation movement because you use only the knee joint to perform it. Although both exercises stress primarily the quadriceps, they will exert stimulus to different areas of the lower body. In most variations of the squat, you will stimulate all the muscles of the quadriceps and provide secondary stress to the muscles of the glutes and hamstrings. You work your entire lower body in this exercise. On the other hand, the leg extension will almost exclusively stress the muscles in the lower part of the quadriceps, particularly in the area of the knee (vastus medialis and vastus lateralis). You will provide only limited stress to the upper portion of the quadriceps (rectus femoris) and virtually no stress to the hamstrings and glutes. Hence, understanding the complexities of compound and isolation exercises is paramount to reaching your training goals. The following paragraphs detail the benefits of compound and isolation movements.

Compound movements are staple exercises in a fitness routine. They help develop your proportions in a way that would be impossible solely by using isolation exercises. They are particularly important in the beginning stages of training, when overall development is your prime concern. Regardless of your level, though, including compound movements in your routine is an absolute necessity. The benefits of these movements include the following:

• *They strengthen the connective tissue supporting your muscles.* If your connective tissue is sufficiently weaker than your muscle tissue, you are prone to tendon and ligament injuries such as pulls, tears, and tendinitis. The connective tissue works in conjunction with your muscles and must be strong for you to progress to the higher levels of training.

• *They help to stimulate many of the smaller muscles that are not specifically targeted by most exercises.* Many of the smaller muscles of the body are not involved in the execution of single-joint movements. These smaller muscles assist in exercise performance and thus help to shape the larger muscles. Moreover, they help add overall detail to your physique and give your body a polished appearance.

• *They provide an efficient means of training the body.* Because you use many different muscles in the performance of a compound movement, you can train with fewer total sets. This is beneficial when you are seeking fundamental development of the muscle or when time constraints do not allow you to split your routine into muscle groups.

As the name implies, isolation movements allow you to isolate specific muscles. An isolation movement uses lighter weights than a compound movement. Because you take supporting muscles out of the movement, the target muscle has to perform almost all the work. As a rule, you should be able to perform about 50 percent of the weight used in a compound movement for the same muscle group. This can vary slightly based on the strength of your primary muscle in a particular exercise. The benefits of isolation movements include the following:

• *They can selectively target a muscle at the exclusion of secondary muscles.* The degree to which you can isolate a particular muscle is somewhat limited. It will be influenced by the location of the muscle and the range of motion of the movement itself. Nevertheless, single-joint exercises are much more concentrated on an individual muscle. Thus, isolation movements tend to be better for advanced bodysculpting and creating muscular symmetry.

• *They put less stress on the connective tissue in comparison with compound movements.* Because you use substantially less weight than you use for compound movements, isolation exercises will reduce the tension applied to the tendons and joints. Hence, they decrease the chance for injury to the connective tissue, one of the most common ailments related to training. This can be of particular benefit when you are training around a previous injury or medical debilitation.

Table 1.2 lists the major muscle groups and some of the corresponding compound and isolation movements. Try to visualize each exercise and understand why it is considered a single- or multi-joint movement. Once you are familiar with this idea, you will be able to determine the origin of almost any exercise and apply it properly in your routine.

Notice that the biceps and triceps were not included in the discussion of compound and isolation movements. These muscles, by nature, involve only one joint. The function of the biceps is to flex the elbow; the triceps extend it. All other

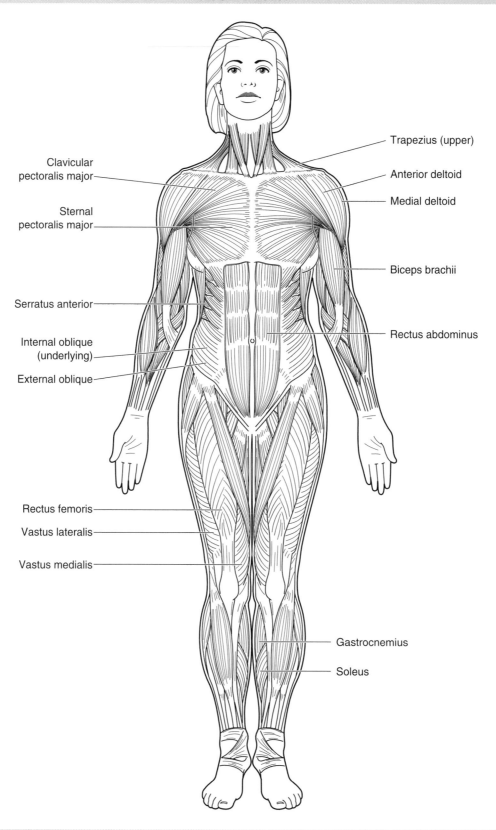

Clavicular
pectoralis major

Sternal
pectoralis major

Serratus anterior

Internal oblique
(underlying)

External oblique

Rectus femoris

Vastus lateralis

Vastus medialis

Trapezius (upper)

Anterior deltoid

Medial deltoid

Biceps brachii

Rectus abdominus

Gastrocnemius

Soleus

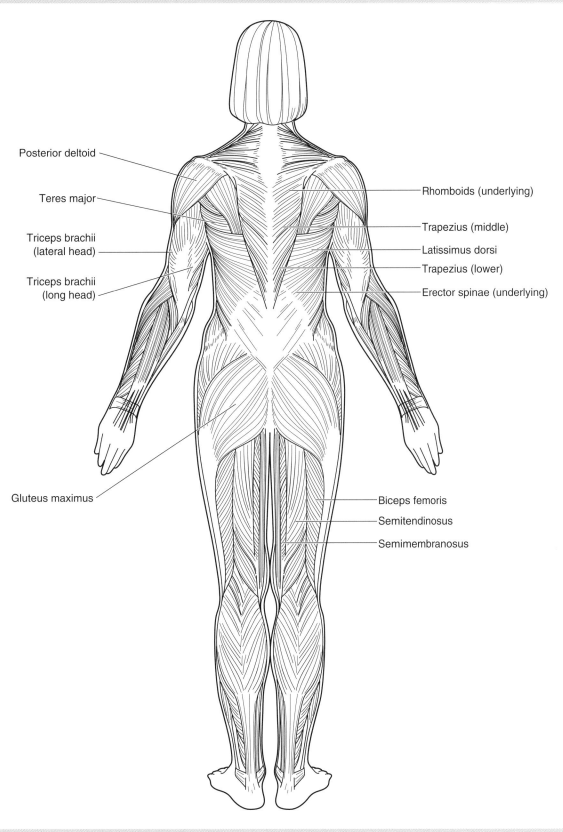

Posterior deltoid

Teres major

Triceps brachii
(lateral head)

Triceps brachii
(long head)

Rhomboids (underlying)

Trapezius (middle)

Latissimus dorsi

Trapezius (lower)

Erector spinae (underlying)

Gluteus maximus

Biceps femoris

Semitendinosus

Semimembranosus

Table 1.2 Compound and Isolation Movements for the Major Muscle Groups

Category	Compound movement	Isolation movement
Back	Lat pulldowns, rows, chins	Pullovers, straight-arm pulldowns
Chest	Presses, push-ups, dips	Flys, pec decks, crossovers
Shoulders	Presses, upright rows	Raises
Quadriceps	Squats, lunges, presses	Extensions, kicks, adductor pulls
Hamstrings and glutes	Good mornings, stiff-legged lifts	Leg curls, abductor pulls

joints must remain stable for proper stimulation. The elbow, therefore, will be the only joint you use in exercises for the arms. Consequently, any exercise for the biceps or triceps is an isolation movement.

Exercise Modalities

Another concept that you should understand is the utility of using several exercise modalities. To achieve maximal definition, you must employ a combination of machines, barbells, dumbbells, cables, and body-weight exercises. Each of these modalities has inherent benefits and drawbacks that make them unique. By selectively combining them into your routine, you can heighten their advantages while minimizing their shortcomings. The following are the various types of modalities and their function in training:

• *Machines*: Among the many types of exercise machines are air-pressure, cam driven, chain link, and so on. Machines generally use a fixed path of movement, forcing you to stay in proper form. This allows you to concentrate on the performance of a set rather than worrying about form. Because controlling the weight stack on a machine requires less skill, you reduce the chance of injury. Moreover, a well-designed machine can provide less resistive force in weaker muscle positions and more force in stronger positions. Hypothetically, this allows you to maximize your strength capabilities, heightening your capacity to define your physique. (Machines, however, do not adapt well to different body types, making this point open for debate.)

• *Dumbbells and barbells*: Also called free weights, barbells and dumbbells are excellent for developing muscular coordination and balance. They provide superb freedom of movement, so you can target individual muscles with better accuracy. Free weights require you to stabilize the weight during exercise performance, activating your secondary muscles and helping to create a polished, symmetrical physique. As a rule, dumbbells are superior to barbells. Dumbbells force both sides of the body to work separately. You therefore apply equal stimulus to each side. By using barbells, the stronger side of your body can compensate for the weaker side. Moreover, dumbbells are more suited to move in line with the natural action of your body, thereby allowing greater range of motion. Accordingly, use dumbbells whenever possible and apply barbells sparingly, mostly for variety.

Weight machines help maximize your strength potential.

- *Cables*: Cables combine some of the benefits of free weights and machines. By providing resistance on both the positive and negative portions of a repetition, they supply continuous tension to your muscles. Because cables can move in three dimensions, they allow you to adapt an exercise to your individual body type (as opposed to a machine, which uses a fixed, two-way movement). Cables are not well suited for compound exercises, so you are, for the most part, restricted to isolation movements.

- *Body-weight exercises*: A body-weight exercise uses your weight, rather than an external weight, for exercise performance. Body-weight exercises can be easy to perform (for example, floor kicks and leg scissors), somewhat strenuous (walking lunges and jump squats), or extremely difficult (chins and sissy squats). Although limited in scope, they are an excellent complement to weight-driven exercises and can be especially beneficial when combined in supersets (which you will learn about later). In the short term, they provide a way to stay in shape when you do not have access to a gym. They are convenient and efficient, and you can perform them almost anywhere.

By combining these modalities, you will have a wealth of exercises from which to choose. Consider the possibilities: you can take an exercise like the biceps curl and perform many different exercises simply by varying the equipment you use to execute the movement. For instance, you could perform seated dumbbell curls, standing barbell curls, rope cable curls, one-arm cable curls, machine curls, one-arm machine curls . . . the list could go on. Open your eyes to the potential for variety and you will improve your development while preventing your workout from going stale.

Setting Goals

To get the most out of this system, you should set short-term fitness goals that will motivate you to train. Most women have good intentions and are brimming with enthusiasm when they begin a fitness routine. Initially, they are eager to go to the gym and are committed to maintaining a regimented program of exercise. Within a short time, however, they begin to lose interest in working out. This usually is due to frustration, but personal issues, feelings of discomfort, impatience, and many other factors can cause enthusiasm to wane.

Dumbbells allow a greater range of motion.

Goal setting is one of the best ways to maintain your motivation to exercise. If you have a clearly defined purpose to train, you are much more likely to continue, and even look forward to, your workout. Of course, everyone has days where they simply do not feel like training. Sickness, family crises, and so forth can affect a person in the short term and decrease the motivation to exercise. If, however, you have well-defined goals that are important to you, you are likely to get back into your routine in short order.

Goals must be both quantifiable and attainable. Goals that do not meet both of these conditions are nonspecific and therefore not meaningful. It is difficult to achieve nonspecific goals, and failure is apt to result in frustration. Let's discuss the qualities of a specific goal in detail:

- *For a goal to be quantifiable, it must have measurable parameters.* For example, losing 20 pounds in three months is a quantifiable goal. You can weigh yourself today and again in three months to see whether you have met your goal. The scale will indicate your weight loss in a measurable context. Other examples of quantifiable goals include reducing your waistline by three inches in a month or dropping one dress size in six weeks. Conversely, wanting to look good is not a quantifiable goal. This is subjective and unmeasurable by any defined standards. A "goal" like this is doomed to lead to disappointment and frustration.

- *For a goal to be attainable, it must be realistic.* For example, losing 20 pounds in three months is an attainable goal. Losing 90 pounds in three months is not. If a goal is not attainable, it can serve as a demotivator. An unattainable goal can make you feel that your training endeavors are pointless. It is better to set modest goals that are readily within reach. Attaining them produces a feeling of accomplishment and spurs you on to loftier goals.

Several techniques are useful in reinforcing your goals and sustaining your motivation to train. One such method is visualization. Visualize your entire body—your arms, legs, shoulders, and so on—and get an image of the way you want it to appear. Think of yourself in great shape, walking on the beach in a bikini or wearing a sexy dress at a party. You might want to think of a woman whose physique you admire and envision yourself developing a comparable body. Let your imagination be your internal source of motivation and, within reason, do not set any boundaries about what you can accomplish.

If you find it difficult to use your imagination as a motivator, find a picture of yourself when you were happy with the way you looked and tape it to the refrigerator or put in on your dresser. It is common to feel you are fighting an uphill battle and lose perspective about your ability to succeed. By having a tangible image in full view, you will reinforce the idea that you have the potential to look terrific. Every time you see this picture it will remind you of your potential!

And I can assure you that if you follow this program, you will soon surpass your previous best.

In short, think about what motivates you and apply it to what you want to get out of your fitness program. You have to ache for something to maintain enthusiasm over time. Without a specific goal, you will not have a reason to put in the work necessary to achieve results. Give yourself an edge and make use of every possible motivator that is meaningful to you—it will inspire you to look good for life.

Once you accomplish a goal, you should immediately set new goals that reflect your mission to work out. This will keep you focused in your efforts and allow you to maintain training ebullience. You should also review your goals periodically to make sure they are consistent with your present objectives. You will often change your goals as you progress in your fitness endeavors. Reevaluating your position can help you stay the course.

Safety Precautions

Finally, you should follow several basic safety precautions in using this program. You cannot improve your physique if an injury prevents you from training. You should observe the following important preventive measures:

Drink plenty of water during training.

• *Get medical clearance before undertaking this program.* Nearly everyone should get a yearly medical checkup to ascertain state of health. If you are over 45 years old, this consideration is mandatory. Heart problems, hypertension, previous surgery, and other conditions can affect your ability to work out. The High-Energy Fitness system is an intense routine that requires much effort. A medical checkup will allow a physician to identify restrictions or contraindications to exercise. If you have a medical condition, you may have to modify this program to accommodate your situation.

• *Take in fluids frequently while training.* You can become dehydrated before your body senses that it needs fluids. You should regularly consume water throughout your workout, drinking every few minutes or so while performing cardiovascular exercise and between each set during weight training. Sports drinks, although much hyped, do not provide additional benefit during exercise. These drinks can furnish short-term energy reserves, but, as long as you maintain a proper nutritional regimen, this point is moot. Moreover, they are generally calorically dense (using simple carbohydrates as their main source of calories), making them counterproductive to achieving optimal definition.

• *Wear a lifting belt during weight training.* Specially designed belts for weightlifting help protect your lower back from undue stress. The lower back is incidentally involved in many exercises and, because it is a vulnerable area, is prone to injury. A lifting belt helps to increase your intra-abdominal pressure, which provides additional support to the muscles of the lower back. Although it will not prevent a lower-back injury, it can alleviate stress to this area and reduce the possibility of minor ailments. You should, however, remove the belt when you perform any abdominal exercises because wearing it will reduce your ability to contract these muscles. It is also advisable to wear lifting gloves during weight training. These specially designed gloves help prevent calluses from forming on your hands—an unsightly blight for many women.

- *Learn to differentiate between soreness and pain.* "No pain, no gain" is a common battle cry in health clubs across the country, but this statement is misleading. Certainly, exercise must be intense and require you to endure some momentary muscular pain. But you must know your body and be able to discriminate between muscular soreness—a natural part of the training process—and pain related to an injury. If you feel sharp pain, stop immediately and see a physician. If you are not sure of the source of the pain, it is better to stop training and wait a day or two before attempting to exercise again. Furthermore, if you feel dizzy during training, take some time to rest. If the dizziness persists, seek medical advice before continuing your routine.

If you have had enough of the theory behind this system, you are in luck! You now know the basics to begin your journey to physique heaven. So put on your sweats, lace up your sneakers, and get ready to start your routine.

2 Warming Up to Training

Many women overlook the importance of warming up before their workout. The warm-up is not glamorous, nor does it appreciably affect the appearance of the body. Women want aesthetic gratification and tend to shun activities that do not produce visible results. This often leads to a tendency to blow off the warm-up and begin training immediately upon entering the gym. When pressed for time, it is usually the first thing discarded from a workout.

The warm-up, however, is an absolute necessity in your workout. It prepares your body for the rigors of intense training by increasing your range of motion, improving your muscular responsiveness, speeding up your recovery, and diminishing the possibility of serious injury. Those who choose to leave this component out of their routines jeopardize their well-being, putting their bodies at risk.

A proper warm-up lasts 10 to 15 minutes and consists of two components—light cardiovascular work and static stretching exercises. In combination, these components ready your body for vigorous exercise. Regardless of your level of experience, your warm-up should remain simple and straightforward. Because the intent is to prepare yourself for intense training, not challenge your resources, advanced techniques and fancy maneuvers are superfluous. Accordingly, whether novice or expert, your warm-up will be about the same. Furthermore, you need not modify it appreciably over time.

Recuperation

Many women think they are augmenting muscle tone as they are working out. Training, in fact, produces the opposite effect. Tiny microscopic tears form in your muscle and connective tissue during training, breaking down muscle tissue. At rest, your body senses that its muscles will soon be stressed again. Thus, the body repairs its muscle tissue to prepare for the next workout. Without rest, the muscles never have a chance to recuperate, and the body may become overtrained. Symptoms of overtraining include insomnia, fatigue, decreased motivation to exercise, flulike symptoms, depression, and increased frequency of injury. If overtraining occurs, you will no longer make gains in training and can even regress in your training efforts.

Because this program is intense, adequate recuperation is essential to repair muscle tissue and avoid overtraining. In most cases, the High-Energy Fitness system works best on a three-day-per-week schedule. Ideally, you should train on nonconsecutive days, thus allowing at least 48 hours for the muscles and central nervous system to regenerate from the previous workout.

Moreover, it is important to listen to your body and make adjustments in your routine based on how you feel. If you are run down, don't hesitate to take an extra day off. If you are disciplined, an extra day or two of rest will not set back your training and can often help to rejuvenate your strength and enthusiasm. When in doubt, it is better to train a little less than to risk overtraining.

If you are really strapped for time, you can still make impressive gains following a two-day-per-week workout schedule. If you choose to train two days per week, it is best to allow 72 hours between workouts (for example, Monday and Thursday). If the two workouts are spaced close together (that is, 48 hours apart), the muscles will have an excessive recuperation period between workouts, diminishing muscular definition. If you decide to follow a two-day-per-week schedule, you should not continue to the targeted body-sculpting phase of the High-Energy Fitness system, which requires a three-day-per-week schedule for optimal results. On a two-day-per-week basis, progress only as far as the toning and shaping phase and attempt to apply some advanced training techniques as you move forward.

Cardiovascular Warm-Up

An excellent way to begin is with a period of light cardiovascular exercise. This increases vascular circulation and elevates body temperature—fundamental preparatory measures for intense exercise. Because the potential for injury is heightened when your body is cold, cardio is the perfect preliminary tool. You can use virtually any cardiovascular activity, including the stationary bike, stairmaster, treadmill, and so forth—the choice is yours. Some women use a variety of activities to reduce boredom, while others prefer to keep their warm-up constant. Either way is fine as long as you meet the basic objective.

Whatever activity you select, you should perform it at relatively low intensity. A rule of thumb is to use a level of approximately 50 percent of your maximal heart rate (220 minus your age), adjusting your intensity as needed. Keep a steady, even tempo and concentrate on maintaining a stable pulse. You should not tax your resources or feel tired or out of breath, either during or after performance. Your goal here is merely to warm your body tissues and accelerate blood flow—not to achieve cardiovascular fitness or reduce body fat. Consequently, if you are at all fatigued from your efforts then you are training too hard! If so, reduce the pace of exercise and continue in a more relaxed fashion. Continue until you break a light sweat (which usually takes about five minutes) and then go on to the next phase.

Stretching

Next, you should employ a period of stretching, lasting for another 5 to 10 minutes. Not only is stretching essential for total fitness, it also helps to counteract some of the debilitating effects of intense weight training. For instance, because your muscles are "shortened" by repetitive contractions during lifting, over time they tend to become taut and less pliant. Consequently, your flexibility decreases, affecting many facets of overall fitness. Moreover, lactic acid and free radicals accumulate in your muscles as a by-product of weight training, decreasing performance and damaging your recuperative capabilities. Stretching helps to offset these impairments, promoting litheness in your muscles and connective tissue, flushing metabolic waste from your body, and alleviating delayed-onset muscle soreness. A great side benefit is that it simply makes you feel good!

Stretching should always be static, using slow, controlled movements. Take extraordinary care to ease into each stretch. Static stretching is the most effective way to achieve flexibility without risking damage to your musculature. It allows for gradual elongation of muscle tissue, permitting you to stretch your body safely to its utmost degree. Again, it is nothing fancy, just an efficient way to accomplish the stated objective.

Although there are those on the fringe who advocate jerky, bouncing maneuvers, you should avoid this dangerous form of stretching. These movements (called ballistic stretching) can easily overload soft-tissue structures beyond their normal elasticity, causing harm to your muscles, joints, and connective tissue. Other experimental forms of stretching, such as proprioceptive neuromuscular facilitation (PNF), have been endorsed but are outside mainstream applications. They have not proven appropriate for general usage and are therefore not ordinarily recommended.

You should stretch your entire body, starting with the lower extremities and working up to the arms and torso. Work all your major muscle groups, regardless of the muscles that you intend to train that day. Give particular attention to areas that tend to be chronically tight, such as your hamstrings, hip flexors, and lower back. Although a single stretching movement is usually all that is necessary for each muscle group, unique considerations, such as an injury or other factors, may require additional attention. When in doubt, spend a little extra time stretching, making sure that you are loose.

When you stretch, go only to the point where you feel tension in the muscle—not to where you experience unbearable pain. If you stretch too far, your body sends a neural impulse to the overstretched muscle (called the stretch reflex), causing it to contract. This reflex tightens the muscle, creating an effect opposite what you are trying to accomplish. By stretching slowly, you can ease into a comfortable zone, taking your body to the edge without going over. As you stretch, keep your body loose and relaxed, breathing in a slow, rhythmic fashion. Hold each move for about 30 seconds, release, and then continue to the next movement.

Some of the many stretches that you can use are demonstrated at the end of this chapter. Although stretching can be an art form, its intricacies are beyond the scope of this book. If you want to know more about stretching and repertoire of movements, consult one of the many books specifically devoted to this subject. Of note is the book *Stretching* by Bob Anderson (1980, Shelter Publications), which delves into the science of stretching and details hundreds of moves, providing many alternatives for each muscle group. Although variation may not be essential in your warm-up, it can create interest in what many consider a tedious part of a workout.

A final comment on stretching is that although it should always be part of your warm-up, you can, if you wish, stretch more often without ill effect. Repeated stretching, unlike weight training, does not diminish your returns; you can achieve additional gains. Because muscle tissue does not break down, your body does not need to recuperate from a stretching session. Moreover, increased volume has been shown to enhance results, promoting better flexibility and dexterity. Stretching is one of the few fitness applications where more really is better!

When you have done both light cardiovasular exercise and stretching, you have completed your warm-up. You can now go on to your workout routine with the confidence that your body is ready for serious training.

Chest Stretch

From a standing position, grasp any stationary object, such as a pole or exercise machine, with your right hand. Your arm should be straight and roughly parallel to the ground. Slowly turn away from the object, allowing your arm to go as far behind your body as comfortably possible. Hold this position for the desired time and repeat the process with your left arm.

Shoulder Stretch

From a standing position, grasp your right wrist with your left hand. Without turning your body, slowly pull your right arm across your torso as far as comfortably possible. Hold this position for the desired time and repeat the process with your left arm.

Lat Stretch

From a standing position, grasp any stationary object, such as a pole or exercise machine, with both hands. Bend your knees and sit back so that your arms are fully extended and supporting your weight. Shift your weight to the right to isolate the right portion of your lat. Hold this position for the desired time and then shift your weight to the left.

Triceps Stretch

From a standing position, raise your right arm over your head. Bend your elbow so that your right hand is behind your head. With your left hand, grasp your right wrist and pull it back as far as comfortably possible, pointing your elbow to the ceiling. Hold this position for the desired time and repeat the process with your left arm.

Biceps Stretch

From a standing position, extend your right arm forward with your palm facing up. Place your left palm underneath your right elbow. Slowly straighten your right arm as much as comfortably possible, pressing your elbow down into your left hand. Hold this position for the desired time and repeat the process with your left arm.

Hamstring Stretch

Sit on the floor with your legs straight and slowly bend forward. Allow your hands to travel down along the line of your body as far as comfortably possible. When you feel an intense stretch in your hamstrings, grab onto your legs and hold this position for the desired time.

Quadriceps Stretch

From a standing position, grasp a stationary object, such as a pole or exercise machine, with your right hand. Bend your left knee and bring your left foot toward your butt. Grasp your left ankle with your left hand and slowly lift your foot as high as comfortably possible. Repeat the process with your right leg.

Calf Stretch

Stand on a raised block of wood, an adjustable step, or other stable surface and grasp a stationary object for balance. Take your right foot off the block so that you are standing on your left leg. Slowly allow your left heel to travel downward as far as comfortably possible. Hold this position for the desired time and repeat the process with your right leg.

3 Body Conditioning

The moment of truth has come! It is time to begin your journey to physique heaven, where you can redefine your body and realize your genetic potential. Until now, I have concentrated on the theory behind the High-Energy Fitness system, theory that will be indispensable in your pursuit of a toned, feminine physique. I have covered many principles and strategies that embody the various facets of fitness. The sooner you combine these mental concepts with the physical aspects of training, the quicker you will reach your goals. Assuming you understand the theoretical basis of the system, you can now put theory into practice. It is best to read this chapter several times before you begin training. By committing the routine to memory you can focus your energy on the training process.

The body-conditioning routine is intended for those who have limited or no training experience. However, even if you have been training for a while, you should use this routine until you are fully confident in your training abilities. When in doubt, it is better to start slowly and assess your ability as you move along. Skip to the next level only if you are prepared for a significant step-up in intensity.

On average, a novice trainee should expect to remain on the body-conditioning routine for three to six months. This may vary depending on individual factors such as initial fitness level, age, athletic ability, and so forth. As you gain experience in training, try to assess your progress dispassionately. The High-Energy Fitness system is set up in a structured format that works in steps. By diligently following the system, you will assure steady improvement. Although it is natural to want to advance quickly, it is counterproductive to go to the next level before you are physically ready. Avoid the trap of seeking instant gratification. In the end, overexuberance will set back your training progress and sabotage your long-term goals.

The High-Energy Fitness system is intended to generate maximal results with minimal potential for injury. Compared with other activities, weight training is a relatively safe endeavor. Still, latent dangers are involved in working out. Studies show that novice trainees are at substantially increased risk of developing ailments related to training. The combination of inexperience and impatience inherent at the beginner level can often lead to overexertion. Thus, the beginner must balance the aspiration to make appreciable gains with the need for safety.

You should realize that weight training can be awkward when you are starting out. Acquiring the various motor skills you need for exercise performance is a laborious process. This can have a negative psychological impact, often decreasing training desire. Be assured, though, that it is normal to feel uncoordinated and clumsy when first training with weights. After all, moving a resistant force through a fixed path, solely by using your muscular strength, is a lofty assignment. Fortunately, within a short time and with continued practice, these skills become second nature. Patience and persistence produce results.

To clarify the goal of the body-conditioning routine, let's revisit the analogy that equates bodysculpting with building a house. As a novice, your aim should be to lay a foundation of muscle on which to build. One of the biggest mistakes women make when they begin a fitness regimen is attempting to shape what they do not have. It is common for a woman to use movements on the inner-thigh machine or butt blaster at the exclusion of all other exercises. Because you cannot spot-reduce body fat (see sidebar), specialized exercises have little value until you develop a base of muscle. A builder cannot begin to construct walls or a roof before a foundation is in place. Similarly, you are the builder of your physique and must develop a foundation that will afford you the greatest potential for sculpting your body.

To build a foundation of muscle, this routine uses a total-body approach to training. You will exercise each major muscle group every time you work out, providing broad-based coverage of your entire body. Total-body training allows you to work each muscle frequently, thereby stimulating a maximal amount of muscle fibers in each training session. You will repeatedly force your entire body to adapt to the stresses of training, helping to achieve overall development.

Initially, the thought of training your entire body every workout is intimidating. This workout is not a cakewalk, but its difficulty is somewhat mitigated by a reduction in the total volume and intensity of the routine. As you will see, the system is configured in a way that optimizes your body's recuperative abilities and builds a foundation of muscle without completely draining your resources. The fol-

Spot Reduction

You cannot spot-reduce fat from your body. I cringe when I see an infomercial for one of the many "ab busters" claiming that you can lose five inches off your waist and drop three dress sizes in a month simply by using their product for five minutes a day. These claims are flagrant misrepresentations that border on consumer fraud. Weight training helps develop shape and hardness in your physique. It cannot make an area of your body smaller, no matter how often or intensely you exercise a given muscle. In the case of the abdominals, training your stomach with crunches, sit-ups, leg raises, or any other abdominal exercise will serve only to increase muscle tone in that area. These exercises will do nothing to flatten your stomach, no matter how hard you try.

lowing is the protocol for the weight-training component of the body-conditioning routine:

- *Exercises:* For each muscle group, you will use only one exercise per training session. Each week you will work your entire body three times. Although training your muscles this frequently can sometimes be overwhelming, the sparseness of the workload will alleviate the risk of overtraining. By performing only one exercise per muscle group, you limit the amount of stress applied to each muscle. This allows you to recuperate quickly from a workout and enables you to train each muscle on a regular basis.

- *Sets:* You should perform three sets of each exercise. This provides ample muscular stimulation without overtaxing the muscles. Do not move from one exercise to the next, as in a circuit routine. Rather, perform one set of an exercise, rest, perform your second set, rest, and then do your third set. This will keep the blood circulating through a muscle group, which increases your muscular "pump" and thereby augments definition. After finishing three sets of an exercise, move on to the next muscle group and perform your subsequent sets in a similar fashion.

- *Rest:* You should rest no more than 30 seconds between sets. This will heighten exercise intensity and increase the aerobic benefit of the workout. In most cases, your routine will take slightly longer in the initial stages of training. As a novice, you will be unfamiliar with the intricacies of training and excessively concerned with matters such as your form, breathing patterns, and so forth. These factors will tend to slow the pace of your training. Still, it is best to keep your rest intervals close to the suggested limits. Rest longer only if you are feeling dizzy or overworked. Your body will quickly adjust to a fast-paced tempo, and you will soon be able to move from one set to the next without incident.

- *Repetitions:* The repetition target will be 15 per set. It is essential to train with good form and to apply continuous tension to your muscles during each repetition. Make an effort to develop your mind-to-muscle link early, making each rep count. From the outset, do not fall into the habit of trying to determine where you are feeling muscular stress. This passive attitude indicates that you are not properly visualizing the target muscle. Rather, think about where you are *supposed* to feel an exercise. Your task is to isolate a muscle or group of muscles, purging all other thoughts. Do not be concerned with your surroundings—whatever might be going on around you is irrelevant. Forget your troubles, your business dealings, your family obligations. Concentrate only on performing each repetition with total focus on your target muscle.

- *Intensity:* You should perform all sets with a weight that is approximately 75 percent of your maximum poundage. Your maximum poundage is defined as a weight that causes you to reach muscular failure on the 15th repetition. A weight of 75 percent of maximum poundage would normally induce momentary muscular failure at 20 repetitions. For example, let's assume that performing leg extensions with 40 pounds causes you to reach failure on the 15th repetition. In this scenario, your working weight for this exercise would be 30 pounds ($40 \times .75$). By your 15th repetition, this weight should begin to feel heavy without causing you to struggle or compromise form to complete the set. As you gain strength, increase the amount of weight to maintain your target of 75 percent of maximum. Moreover, as you gain experience, you can gradually increase the percentage of maximum weight to a point where you begin to approach failure (going as high

Conditioning Protocols

Number of exercises:	1 per muscle group
Number of sets:	3 per exercise
Rest between sets:	No more than 30 seconds
Repetitions per set:	15
% of maximum weight	75%

as 90 percent of maximum poundage). This can help prepare your body for the intensity required in the next level of training. It is not advisable, though, to attempt to train to absolute failure. Your body is not yet geared for such intense exercise, and you will invariably become overtrained.

The element in the left margin summarizes the specific protocols of the body-conditioning phase of this system. Follow these protocols rigidly, with little modification. As you become familiar with the training process and progress to the more advanced phases of this system, you will have flexibility to alter the structure of the routine. At this level, however, it is best to keep things simple.

Using a training diary can help you move smoothly through your routine. A good strategy is to write down in advance the exercises that you will perform. You can then do your workout routine knowing exactly what you are supposed to accomplish in the session. In this way, you won't aimlessly wander around thinking about which exercises to perform. The diary should include the exercises you used in each session, the amount of weight that you used in each set, and any notes that might help you in the future.

If you have never trained before, or have not trained for some time, consider your first few workouts an acclimation period. The goal should be to adapt your body to the routine and allow it to adjust to the stresses of weight training. Although you are probably already eager to see results, you should approach this phase as if you were about to swim in a cold pool. Obviously, it would be ill advised to dive headfirst into the pool without first testing the water! Your body could go into shock from the extreme difference between body temperature and the temperature of the water. Similarly, your muscles, connective tissue, and nervous system will experience shock from the demands of training, making it easy to overtax your body during this fragile period. If you are not careful, you can experience severe soreness, headaches, or injuries from overzealous efforts. These ailments can set back or stop your ability to work out—and limit your potential to achieve results. Nothing can derail your workout regimen more than an injury, so use discretion.

Moreover, conditions related to age can further inhibit initial training efforts. After the age of 35, a woman loses roughly 1 percent of her muscle mass and bone density each year. By age 45, a woman will have lost about 10 percent of her fundamental body mass, by 55, 20 percent, and so on. Because this progression compromises strength and endurance, your capacity to train at an intense level will, at first, be hampered. Consequently, the older you are, the more careful you should be to acclimate your body during the initial stages of training. Although you can reverse the effects of aging, it will take time and a dose of patience.

To acclimate your body, you should use only 50 percent of your maximum weight during your first training session. In each successive workout, you can gradually increase the poundage until you reach your target weight. Determining your starting weight requires you to estimate your initial strength level, but without physically training to failure, you can only make an educated guess of your lifting abilities. To prevent injury, err on the side of caution and choose a

Patience is needed to reverse the physical effects of aging.

weight that is too light rather than too heavy. Remember, this is only an acclimation period, and you need not push hard. You will soon be able to gauge your strength and know beforehand the weight required for a particular exercise.

Even with proper acclimation, you should expect to feel a degree of muscular soreness. This is especially prevalent in the first few weeks of training, but you will experience this malady even after becoming an accomplished trainee. Although the pain should not be severe, you should feel tenderness and sensitivity in the muscles that you trained. Unfortunately, soreness is a necessary by-product of the training process. It arises from microscopic tears that occur from the stress of weight training, which subsequently cause internal swelling in your muscles and connective tissue. Usually, the soreness will last several days and slowly subside as your body initiates the healing process. This is an indication that your body is adapting to the demands of exercise and preparing itself for the next training session.

It is important that you not let muscular soreness inhibit or deter your training efforts. Working out during periods of mild soreness can help assuage the associated pain and discomfort. Training aids the circulation of blood flow through your muscles and connective tissue, which can accelerate recuperation. If you are extremely uncomfortable and simply cannot train, take a few days off and use soothing remedies such as whirlpool baths to alleviate the soreness. Try not to stay completely sedentary, though; even mild activity can increase circulation to body tissue and accelerate the healing process. Of course, if you experience any sharp pain, stop training immediately and seek the advice of a physician.

During the initial four- to six-week training period, you should employ compound movements whenever possible. As previously discussed, compound movements will stimulate the greatest amount of muscle fibers, as well as strengthen your connective tissue and orient your nervous system to the demands of weight training. This will help you achieve balanced development from the outset and negate the possibility of developing muscular deficiencies as you progress in your endeavors. The many variations of compound exercises permit you to add variety to your training and still meet this directive.

Table 3.1 details a three-day sample routine that you might use in the first four to six weeks of your routine. These routines, like all the sample routines in this book, are only a guide to the possibilities of creating a diversified workout. A multitude of combinations is available for you to explore. Varying your routine will optimize results and help prevent boredom.

It is important to note the order of the exercises and how they relate to each muscle group. In the beginning stages of training, it is best to train large muscle groups first in your routine. Although it does not really matter whether you train your upper or lower body first, you should train the muscles of the torso (chest,

Table 3.1 Conditioning Program Three-Day Sample Routine

Muscle group	Day 1	Day 2	Day 3
Chest	Incline dumbbell presses	Machine chest presses	Push-ups
Back	Front lat pulldowns	Seated rows	One-arm dumbbell rows
Shoulders	Military presses	Arnold presses	Upright rows
Biceps	Seated dumbbell curls	Cable curls	EZ curls
Triceps	Nosebreakers	Pushdowns	Close-grip bench presses
Quadriceps	Leg presses	Squats	Lunges
Hamstrings and glutes	Good mornings	Stiff-legged deadlifts	Hyperextensions
Calves	Seated calf raises	Donkey calf raises	Standing calf raises
Abdominals	Crunches	Bench leg raises	Knee-ins

back, and shoulders) before the arms (biceps and triceps) and the muscles of the quadriceps before the hamstrings. If you train smaller muscles first, they will be less able to serve as secondary muscle movers in exercises for the larger muscle groups. Ultimately, your secondary muscles will fatigue before your primary muscles, and you will not achieve maximal stimulation of the target muscle. For instance, performing a barbell curl will exhaust your biceps. If you then perform a seated row, your biceps will tend to give out before you fully stimulate the muscles of your back, thereby decreasing the effectiveness of the exercise.

Moreover, when training the upper body, it is best to alternate between pushing and pulling movements. The chest, shoulders, and triceps are used to push a weight, while the back and biceps are pulling mechanisms. Alternating these movements allows several minutes for the antagonist muscle to rest, thereby improving energy resources for exercise performance. Notice in the sample routine that you train first the chest (which uses the shoulders and triceps as secondary muscle movers), next the back (which uses the biceps), then the shoulders (which use the triceps), and finally the biceps and triceps. In this way, you maximize muscular recovery between each exercise.

After the initial four- to six-week acclimation phase, you should begin to incorporate isolation movements into your routine. Experiment with different exercises, paying close attention to the unique qualities of each movement. Make sure, though, that you do not neglect to include compound movements in your workout. These staple exercises, because of their all-encompassing effect, have great utility for beginners. Mixing a variety of compound and isolation movements into your workout will serve as a precursor to the next level of training, in which you will use a split routine.

Table 3.2 shows a three-day sample routine that expands on the initial routine by combining a variety of compound and isolation movements. You should now be comfortable with the structure of this routine and should work on perfecting what you have learned. Again, be creative and do not be afraid to try new exercises. This will not only provide stress to a maximum number of muscle fibers but also hone your performance skills for future gain.

When executing unilateral movements (in which you train one arm or leg at a time), it is best to avoid resting between sets. In the one-arm dumbbell row, for

Table 3.2 Three-Day Routine With Compound and Isolation Movements

Muscle group	Day 1	Day 2	Day 3
Chest	Pec decks	Flat dummbell presses	Flat bench flys
Back	Reverse lat pulldowns	One-arm seated rows	Straight-arm pulldowns
Shoulders	Shoulder presses	Lateral raises	Bent lateral raises
Biceps	Preacher curls	Incline curls	Concentration curls
Triceps	Triceps kickbacks	Triceps dips	Overhead extensions
Quadriceps	Leg extensions	Hack squats	Front squats
Hamstrings and glutes	Lying leg curls	Abductor pulls	Seated leg curls
Calves	Seated calf raises	Toe presses	Donkey calf raises
Abdominals	Rope crunches	Hanging leg raises	Twisting crunches

instance, you should start with one arm, perform 15 repetitions, go to the other arm, perform 15 repetitions, and repeat this process without rest. Thus, one side will be able to recuperate while you use the other for performance of the movement. By the time that you have completed 15 repetitions on one side, your alternate side should be fully recovered and ready to continue with the set. Because your body is never totally at rest, you will be able to maintain an accelerated heart rate, increasing your body's ability to burn fat.

As you try different exercises, you will probably find some movements uncomfortable or awkward to perform. There may be several causes for this. Sometimes, even after repeated attempts, an exercise will just not feel right to you. If this is the case, simply drop it from your routine and move on to a complementary movement. There is no reason to keep the exercise in your training arsenal. You may decide, however, to try the exercise again after you have further developed your strength and motor skills. Often, you ultimately will find the movement to be natural and realize additional benefits from added variety.

You might wonder what to do if you are not able to perform a complete set of 15 repetitions of a particular exercise. In most cases, you should be able to decrease the weight enough so that you can achieve your target rep number. But you will probably come upon an exercise that, no matter how hard you try, will defeat your effort to finish an entire set. This may especially be true in abdominal exercises and other body-weight-influenced movements, in which your own weight will affect your strength capabilities. If you just cannot attain 15 reps for a given set, perform as many repetitions as you can until your body gives out. Fortunately, strength and endurance tend to build up quickly, and you will see rapid improvement in these areas. With continued effort, you should be able to achieve your target repetition number on virtually any exercise.

Once you have used the body-conditioning routine for a while, you will probably reach a point where you feel that you are ready to advance to a higher level. Understand, though, that taking the next step involves a significant increase in discipline and intensity. Each subsequent level of training requires a greater amount of effort. You therefore must use discretion in going forward. You may then wonder "How do I know when I am ready to take the next step?" In truth, there is no certain answer. Before you continue, however, you should consider these points:

• *Make sure that you are knowledgeable about the basic principles of exercise.* The mental aspects of training become increasingly important as you climb the ladder in your fitness endeavors. Understanding these principles will be crucial in maximizing results at the next level of training. Make sure that you are clear on each principle and understand how they apply to the training process.

• *Make sure that you are comfortable with a variety of compound and isolation exercises.* You should be able to perform dozens of exercises and be able to move easily from one to the next. Moreover, you should have a good grasp of exercise form and function and know the muscles that each exercise will target. In the next level of training, this knowledge will allow you to combine these movements to mesh synergistically with one another.

• *Make sure that you are willing and able to increase your exercise intensity.* It is one thing to want to train on a more advanced basis; it is another to endure the intensity required for this progression. Many women do not realize the increased effort required to train at the next level. The body-conditioning routine is preparation for developing overall intensity. You should gauge your ability to progress based on the difficulty you have with this routine.

If you are still not proficient or capable in any of these areas, take more time to develop your skills and mental acuity. Work on the basics, preparing your mind and body for more intense training. Do not pressure yourself to advance to the next phase. In fact, if you are happy with the way that you look at this point, you can continue with the body-conditioning phase indefinitely. Many women do not aspire, or are not willing, to train at a higher pace and are content with maintaining the status quo. This routine, however, will not advance you to your genetic potential. Therefore, if you want to take the next step and begin the process of bodysculpting, advance to chapter 4 and read on.

Lori Dean: Star of ESPN2's "Crunch Fitness"

Height: 5'5 1/2"

Weight: 135

P.O. Box 3818, Minneapolis, MN 55403

Many women are extremely intimidated by the prospect of lifting weights. They adhere to misconceptions about the effects of weight training and often avoid any type of strength-related activity. As a teenager, Lori Dean shared many of these beliefs. "During high school, I was discouraged from weight training by my physical education coaches. They were constantly telling me, 'Make sure you use really light weights or you'll get too big.' So, as a young, impressionable girl, I was scared to seriously get into lifting. The social angle plays a big role when you're young, and I thought that weights would make me bulky and unattractive."

Photo courtesy of Lori Dean

It wasn't until she entered college that Laurie embraced the weight room. "Around the age of 20, I started teaching aerobics and several of the other aerobics teachers were heavily into weight training. I saw how hard these women were training and noticed that they looked great. They were very strong and fit but maintained their femininity. So I decided that I'd give it a try and see how my body responded."

Laurie admits that it took a while to overcome her apprehension. "At the beginning, I was still a little hesitant about pushing myself to the limit. It was difficult for me to accept that I could really train hard without getting bulky. But the more I trained, the more I realized that women don't have the capacity to gain significant muscular size. As long as you train in the proper fashion, bulking up isn't a concern. Once I got comfortable with this realization, I really went all out in my training approach and the results were fantastic."

Despite her initial misgivings, Lori now is one of the biggest advocates of weight training for women. "Weight training has made a huge difference in my strength and appearance. It's a shame that so many women have preconceived notions that inhibit them realizing the benefits that it affords. I can say from experience that none of these myths have any credence."

Lori's training tip

"It's never too early or too late to start an exercise program. Fitness can benefit everyone, no matter what your age."

Chest Exercises

INCLINE DUMBBELL PRESSES

Lie on an incline bench set at approximately 30 to 40 degrees, your feet firmly planted on the floor, a dumbbell in each hand. With your palms turned away from you, bring the dumbbells to shoulder level so that they rest just above your armpits. Press both dumbbells over your chest, moving them toward each other so that the sides of the dumbbells gently touch. Feel a contraction in your chest at the top of the movement. Return to the starting position.

Flat Dumbbell Presses

Follow the directions for incline dumbbell presses, except lie on a flat bench instead of one set at an incline.

Chest Exercises

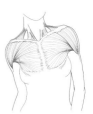

INCLINE MACHINE CHEST PRESSES

Sit in a chest press machine, aligning your upper chest with the machine handles. Grasp the handles with a shoulder-width grip, your palms facing away from you. Slowly press the handles forward, stopping just before your elbows fully lock. Feel a contraction in your chest at the end of the movement. Return to the starting position.

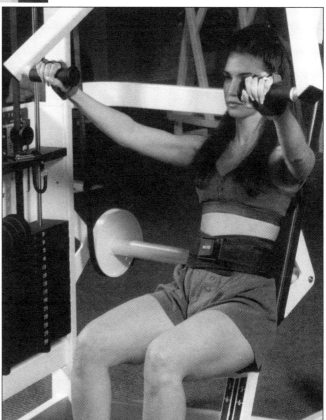

Chest Exercises

PUSH-UPS

Plant your hands and toes on the floor. Keep your torso and legs rigid, holding your back perfectly straight through the move. Bend your arms and slowly lower your body, stopping just before your upper chest touches the ground. Feel a stretch in your chest. Push up to the starting position.

Chest Exercises

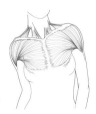

PEC DECK FLYS

Place your forearms on the pads of a pec deck machine. Your elbows should press into the pads and your back should remain immobile through the movement. Press the pads together, gently touching them directly in front of your chest. Hold this position for two counts while contracting your chest muscles. Slowly return to the starting position.

Chest Exercises

FLAT BENCH FLYS

Lie on a flat bench, planting your feet firmly on the floor. Grasp two dumbbells and hold them to the sides, keeping a slight bend at your elbows through the move. Your palms should face in and toward the ceiling, and your upper arms should be roughly parallel with the bench. Slowly raise the weights in a semicircle, as if you were hugging a large tree. Gently touch the weights at the top of the move. After feeling a contraction in your chest, return to the starting position.

Back Exercises

SEATED ROWS

Grasp a V-bar attached to a low pulley with your palms facing each other. Place your feet against the footplate and, keeping a slight bend in your knees, sit down in front of the pulley. Fully straighten your arms so that you feel a complete stretch in your lats. Slowly pull the V-bar to your lower abdomen, keeping your elbows close to your sides. As the handle touches your body, arch your lower back and squeeze your shoulder blades together. Return to the starting position.

Back Exercises

ONE-ARM SEATED ROWS

Grasp a loop attached to a low pulley with your left hand. Place your feet against the footplate and, keeping a slight bend in your knees, sit down in front of the pulley. Fully straighten your arm so that you feel a complete stretch in your left lat. Slowly pull the loop to your lower left side, keeping your elbow in at all times. As you reach the finish position, arch your lower back and contract your left lat. Return to the starting position. Repeat with your right arm after finishing the desired reps on your left.

Back Exercises

ONE-ARM DUMBBELL ROWS

Place your left hand and left knee on a flat bench, planting your right foot firmly on the floor. Your torso should be parallel to the ground through the entire movement. Grasp a dumbbell in your right hand with your palm facing you and let it hang by your side. Keeping your elbow close to your body, pull the dumbbell upward and back until it touches your hip. Feel a contraction in your upper back. Lower the dumbbell to the starting position. Repeat with your left arm after finishing the desired reps on your right.

Shoulder Exercises

MILITARY PRESSES

Sit at the edge of a flat bench. Grasp a barbell with your palms facing away from you and bring it to your upper chest. Slowly press the barbell directly over your head, contracting your deltoids at the top of the move. Slowly return to the starting position.

Shoulder Exercises

ARNOLD PRESSES

Sit on the edge of a flat bench. Grasp two dumbbells with your palms facing you and bring the weights to shoulder level. Press the dumbbells directly up, simultaneously rotating your hands so that your palms face forward during the last portion of the movement. Touch the weights together over your head. Slowly lower the dumbbells, rotating your hands, to the starting position.

Shoulder Exercises

UPRIGHT ROWS

Using a shoulder-width, overhand grip, grasp a bar attached to a low pulley. Relax your arms at your sides and stand comfortably with your knees slightly bent. Slowly lift the bar along the line of your body until it approaches your chin, keeping your elbows higher than your wrists at all times. Contract your delts. Slowly lower the bar to the starting position.

Biceps Exercises

SEATED DUMBBELL CURLS

Sit at the edge of a flat bench. Grasp a pair of dumbbells with your hands facing away from you and hold them at your sides. Press your elbows into your sides and keep them stable through the move. Slowly curl the dumbbells toward your shoulders, contracting your biceps at the top of the move. Return to the starting position.

Biceps Exercises

CABLE CURLS

Using a palms-up, shoulder-width grip, grasp a straight bar attached to a low pulley. Maintain a slight bend to your knees and press your elbows to your sides, stabilizing them through the move. Slowly curl the bar toward your shoulders and contract your biceps at the top of the move. Return to the starting position.

Biceps Exercises

CONCENTRATION CURLS

Sit at the edge of a flat bench with your legs wide apart. Grasp a dumbbell in your right hand and brace your right triceps on the inside of your right knee. Straighten your arm so that it hangs near the floor. Slowly curl the weight up and in along the line of your body, contracting your biceps at the top of the move. Return to the starting position. Repeat with your left arm after finishing the desired reps on your right.

Triceps Exercises

NOSEBREAKERS

Lie on a flat bench, your feet planted firmly on the floor. Grasp an EZ-curl bar with your palms facing away from you and straighten your arms so that the bar is directly over your chest. Keeping your elbows in and pointed toward the ceiling, slowly lower the bar until the weights are just above the level of your forehead. Press the bar up until it reaches starting position.

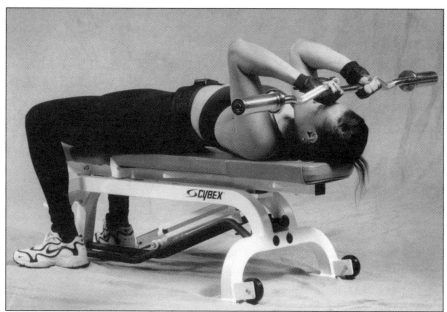

Triceps Exercises

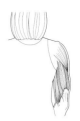

TRICEPS PRESSDOWNS

Using an overhand grip, grasp a straight bar attached to a high pulley. Stand with your feet shoulder-width apart with your knees slightly bent and your torso angled forward. Bend your arms so that your elbows form a 90-degree angle. Keeping your elbows at your sides, slowly straighten your arms, contracting your triceps. Return to the starting position.

One-Arm Reverse Pressdowns

Follow the directions for triceps pushdowns, except use a loop attachment on the high pulley, grasping it in a palms-up grip, and isolate your right arm first. Repeat with your left arm after finishing the desired reps on your right.

Triceps Exercises

CLOSE-GRIP BENCH PRESSES

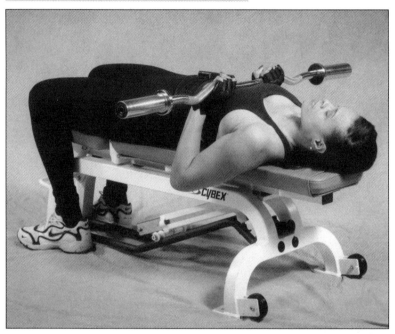

Lie on a flat bench with your feet planted firmly on the floor. Grasp an EZ-curl bar with your hands approximately six to eight inches apart. Bring the bar directly under your pecs. Keeping your elbows close to your sides, slowly press the weight straight up, contracting your triceps. Return to the starting position.

Quadriceps Exercises

LEG PRESSES

Sit in a leg press machine, pressing your back firmly into the padded seat. Place your feet shoulder-width apart on the footplate. Straighten your legs and unlock the carriage release bars. Slowly bring your knees to your chest. Without bouncing at the bottom, press the weight up, stopping just before your knees lock. Contract your quads. Return to the starting position.

Quadriceps Exercises

SQUATS

Rest a straight bar high on the back of your neck. Stand with your feet shoulder-width apart, grasping the bar with both hands. Slowly lower your body until your thighs are parallel with the ground. Slightly arch your lower back and keep your heels on the floor at all times. When you reach a "seated" position, straighten your legs and return to the starting position.

Front Squats

Follow the directions for squats, except rest the straight bar across your chest, holding it in place with both hands.

Quadriceps Exercises

HACK SQUATS

Stand in a hack squat machine with the upper pads on your shoulders. Stand with your feet shoulder-width apart and slightly in front. Unlock the carriage release bars and slowly lower your body until your thighs are parallel with the ground, keeping your heels down at all times. When you reach a "seated" position, straighten your legs and return to the starting position.

Hamstring-Glute Exercises

GOOD MORNINGS

Rest a barbell across your shoulders, grasping the bar on both sides to maintain balance. Stand with your feet shoulder-width apart and keep your lower back taut through the movement. Slowly bend forward until your torso is roughly parallel to the floor. Slowly control yourself up, contracting your glutes as you return to the starting position.

Hamstring-Glute Exercises

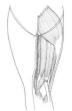

STIFF-LEGGED DEADLIFTS

Stand with your feet shoulder-width apart. Grasp a straight bar and let it hang in front of your body. Keeping your knees straight, slowly bend forward and lower the barbell until you feel an intense stretch in your hamstrings. Contract your glutes as you return to the starting position.

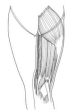

Hamstring-Glute Exercises

LYING LEG CURLS

Lie face-down on a lying leg curl machine with your heels hooked under the roller pads. Keeping your thighs pressed to the machine, slowly curl your feet, stopping just short of your butt or as far as comfortably possible. Contract your hamstrings. Return to the starting position.

Seated Leg Curls

Follow the directions for lying leg curls, except use a seated leg curl machine. Lower the leg restraint over your thighs to secure them. Slowly press your feet down as far as comfortably possible, contracting your hamstrings when your knees are fully bent.

Calf Exercises

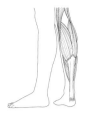

TOE PRESSES

Sit in a leg press machine, your back firmly pressed into the padded seat. Place your toes a comfortable distance apart on the bottom of the footplate. Straighten your legs, unlock the carriage release bars, and drop your heels below your toes. Keeping your knees stable, slowly press your toes as high up as you can. Contract your calves. Slowly return to the starting position.

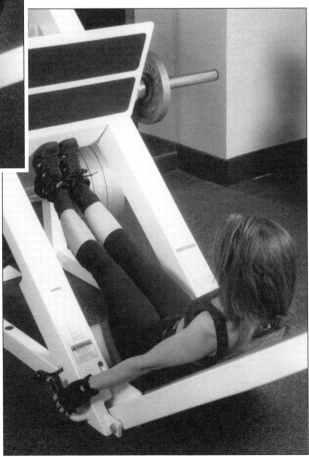

Abdominal Exercises

CRUNCHES

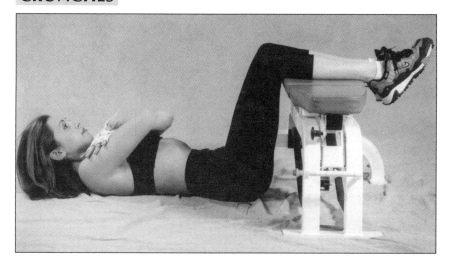

Lie on the floor with your calves resting on a flat bench. Keep your thighs perpendicular to the ground and fold your hands across your chest. Slowly raise your shoulders toward your knees. Feel a contraction in your abdomen. Slowly return to the starting position.

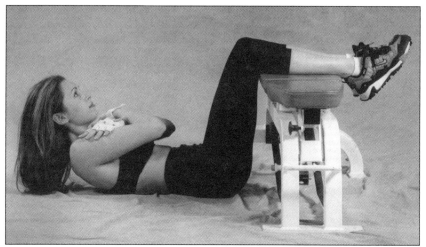

Twisting Crunches

Follow the directions for crunches, except as you raise your shoulders toward your knees, twist to the right. Repeat by twisting to the left after finishing the desired reps to the right.

Abdominal Exercises

BENCH LEG RAISES

Sit at the edge of a flat bench. Keep your upper torso at a 45-degree angle above the bench, your feet straight out and slightly below the bench. Maintaining a stable upper body, slowly raise your legs to a 45-degree angle to the floor. Contract your abs. Slowly lower your legs, returning to the starting position.

Abdominal Exercises

KNEE-INS

Sit at the edge of a flat bench. Keep your upper torso at a 45-degree angle above the bench, your feet straight out. Simultaneously bring your upper torso and knees toward each other, as if you were curling into a ball. Contract your abs and then slowly uncurl your body, returning to the starting position.

4 Toning and Shaping

Congratulations, you are no longer a beginner! By maintaining your fitness regimen, you have surpassed the efforts of more than 80 percent of the population. You should already see some fairly substantial changes taking place in your physique. It is important to realize, though, that you have only achieved about 50 percent of your genetic potential. Your journey has just begun. In this routine, you will begin to shape and refine the muscle that you have amassed.

The toning and shaping phase of this system is your entrée into bodysculpting. You have already built a foundation to your physique. You must now concentrate on erecting a frame. This entails bringing your body into aesthetic proportion and creating symmetry between your muscles. Each muscle group should flow into the next, creating balanced lines that complement one another. You should begin to assess your strengths and weaknesses, becoming in tune with the intricacies of your body.

This routine incorporates several changes to further your results. For one, the total volume of exercises and sets that you perform for each muscle group will increase. This will allow you to work a muscle more intensively, improving your prospects for shape and tone. Accordingly, your muscles will need a greater recuperation period to repair the effects of this added stress. Thus, you will split your workout into two parts: you will train half your body in one workout and the other half in the next workout. The net effect is that you will train each muscle group three times every two weeks (instead of three times a week, as in the body-conditioning routine), giving your body twice as much recuperation as before.

On average, you should expect to remain on this routine for at least six months. Continue to be patient about your expectations for improving your physique. As previously noted, this program works in a systematic fashion. You will make gains on a steady, if not spectacular, basis. Thus, do not attempt to progress to the next level before you are physically and mentally ready for the challenge. Doing so will invariably inhibit your long-term progress.

As always, you should warm up thoroughly before each training session. Because you will work only half of your body each session, be sure to warm up the specific muscles that you will be training. This routine will be substantially more intense than the previous one, so an adequate warm-up is imperative to prevent injury.

After your warm-up, go directly to the weight-training portion of your program. As your fitness goals and capabilities evolve, you must adapt your routine to meet your changing needs. This is the only way you can move forward and avoid reaching a training plateau. To help you take the next step, employ the following protocols for this phase of your weight-training routine:

• *Exercises:* You should use two exercises for each muscle group (as opposed to one in the body-conditioning routine). This will allow you to work your muscles from different angles and lines of pull in the same training session, augmenting your bodysculpting potential. You should use one compound movement and one isolation movement for each muscle group. (Of course, this is not feasible in the arms, calves, or abdominals because they involve a single joint.) By combining exercises in this way, your muscles will receive complete development.

• *Sets:* You will again perform three sets for each exercise. Because you are now using two exercises for each muscle group, you perform a total of six sets for each major muscle (in the body-conditioning routine you performed only three sets). Initially, this increase in training volume will promote significant muscular fatigue. You should expect to have reduced energy levels for several weeks until your body adapts to this extended workload. Within a short time, though, your body will adjust to these demands, and your exercise tolerance will improve dramatically.

• *Rest:* As in the body-conditioning phase, you should rest no more than 30 seconds between sets. Because limited rest intervals are one of the primary factors in generating an aerobic effect on your body, it is paramount to train in an expeditious fashion. This will heighten your fat-burning capabilities as well as diminish the possibility of adding muscular bulk.

• *Repetitions:* The target repetition number will continue to be 15 per set. However, although you will use 15 repetitions as a goal, you might fall short of this number as you advance your efforts. Your objective is to develop your body—not lift a weight 15 times. The easiest thing you can do is choose a light weight that you can comfortably lift 15 times. Instead, you should aim to push your body to the outer limits of what you can handle. Fifteen is not a magic number—it is simply a "toning target." Whether you ultimately complete 14 or 16 repetitions is irrelevant as long as you are maximally stimulating your muscles within this range.

• *Intensity:* The routine includes a progression of intensity in which each successive set will require more effort. As in the body-conditioning routine, perform your first set at approximately 75 percent of your maximum weight. On the second set, you should increase intensity to approximately 90 percent (which will approach

Intensity

Intensity is a key component of High-Energy Fitness. To accelerate the fat-burning process and eliminate the potential of building excessive muscle mass, this system takes an aerobic approach to weight training. You accomplish this by generating high intensity during the training phase of the program through limited rest intervals and training to muscular failure.

In bodysculpting, intensity is defined as the amount of work performed in a given time. You can heighten intensity in two ways—by increasing the weight you use or by decreasing the rest interval between sets. High-Energy Fitness uses a target rest interval of 20 to 30 seconds between sets, which is considered an accelerated training pace. This will elevate your heart rate to optimize fat burning while allowing enough time for your body to recover and generate sufficient intensity for the next set.

Once you progress in your bodysculpting endeavors, High-Energy Fitness mandates that you train to muscular failure. This means that the last repetition of a set should be extremely difficult, if not impossible, to perform. Weight training is one of the few activities in which failure is a desired outcome. This is a strange concept to grasp. We live in a society that rewards us for our accomplishments and punishes us for our failures. From the time we are born, we are urged to succeed. We think of failure as an unacceptable alternative. But in this system, weight training is a means to an end. Your goal should be not to attain a given number of repetitions but to develop a lean, toned physique. Training to failure within the context of High-Energy Fitness will induce maximal stress on a muscle while initiating an aerobic effect on the body. This will promote the dual benefit of burning fat for fuel while improving muscular shape and definition.

One of the side benefits of this approach is that it dramatically decreases the amount of time that you need to train. Only a few sets of an exercise are required to stimulate maximal muscular stress. Once you completely overload a muscle, additional training becomes superfluous. Combined with a rapid training pace, High-Energy Fitness is an efficient method for expediting gains with a minimal commitment of time.

failure). Finally, on your third set, you should go all out: by your 15th repetition, you should reach momentary muscular failure and not be able to get even one more repetition. By the end of your last set, your target muscle should be completely fatigued, and you should perform your next exercise in the same fashion.

The element in the margin of the next page summarizes the specific protocols of the toning and shaping phase of this system. As discussed above, you will have some added flexibility in certain aspects of your routine. For the most part, however, you should rigidly follow these protocols to generate optimal results. You are still learning your body at this point; deviating from the basic protocols can lead to overtraining or injury, setting back your training endeavors.

Perhaps the biggest change between the body-conditioning routine and this routine is an increase in intensity. As a beginner, you were merely building a foundation for your physique. Thus, the intensity of your workout was less of an issue. Because your body was not acclimated to the training process, working out with too much intensity could have led to overtraining. If you truly strive to redefine your body, however, you must work harder to get where you want to go. Television commercials that show women with great bodies smiling as they daintily lift weights are pure fantasy. Sculpting a great body involves effort. You will gasp and sweat to get there.

As noted, you will gradually increase intensity until you are training to momentary muscular failure. From a training perspective, failure equals success! When you first attempt to train to failure, it can be both a confusing and an enlightening experience—one that you might not be prepared to endure. While lifting a weight, most women are prone to give up mentally before their muscles truly give out. They

Toning Protocols

Number of exercises:	2 per muscle group
Number of sets:	3 per exercise
Rest between sets:	No more than 30 seconds
Repetitions per set:	15
% of maximum weight	1st set—75%, 2nd set—90%, 3rd set—failure

may think they have induced muscular failure, yet their muscles are capable of completing several more repetitions. To obtain the best results, you must learn to differentiate between mental failure and physical failure. Remember the adage "If it doesn't kill you, it will make you stronger." By pushing yourself to the limit, your internal and external strength will show itself, allowing your body to achieve more than you ever could have imagined.

To ready your body for the increase in intensity, this routine uses a set progression for muscular acclimation. Your first two sets will prepare you for your final, all-out set. Each set is more intense until you reach momentary muscular failure on your last set. Because you will not have another set for which to save your energy, you can push yourself to the limit without worrying about preserving your strength reserves. When I train a client, I use the motto "Last set, best set!" meaning that you should expend all your resources in completing your final set. By progressively adapting your workload, you will have ample endurance to push hard without overtraining your body.

Of course, along with this increase in intensity, you should expect to experience more mental and physical discomfort. Although most of us seek to avoid pain, it is unfortunately an unavoidable and necessary by-product of the training process. Intense training places significant stress on your muscles and taxes your entire nervous system. This in itself produces an uncomfortable effect on your body. As you approach muscular failure, your body secretes a waste product called lactic acid that not only brings about muscular fatigue but also causes a burning sensation in the muscles you are training. Your body is likely to quiver as you struggle to complete your final reps. (This is caused by your Golgi tendon reflex threshold, which is a protective response to muscular overload.) All of these responses act against your mental will, challenging you to give up.

When these physiological responses occur, you must be mentally strong enough to think beyond your discomfort. The pain that you endure while training is short-lived and will subside within seconds of completing your set. Thus, when training to failure, rationalize that it will be over momentarily, ignoring your pain threshold. Realize that once your set is complete, you will have the satisfaction of setting yourself on a course to achieve the body of your dreams. You will be sacrificing short-term satisfaction for long-term gain—a worthy payoff!

Now that the protocols have been established, you may be wondering about the best way to incorporate them into a cohesive training regimen. You can combine muscle groups into a practical split routine in many different ways. One such possibility is blending agonist-antagonist muscle groups in the same session. Agonist-antagonist muscle groups are those whose actions directly oppose one another. For example, the biceps and triceps are agonist-antagonist muscles. When you contract your biceps by flexing your arm (thereby shortening your biceps), your triceps work in an opposing fashion, limiting the contraction (thereby lengthening the triceps). Because blood flow is centralized to this entire area, combining these muscles in the same workout can increase the benefits of vascular circulation. Table 4.1 illustrates sample routines that combine agonist-antagonist muscle groups into a cohesive workout. Remember that these sample routines are only a guide. Feel free to vary your routine each time you work out.

Table 4.1 Sample Routines Combining Agonist and Antagonist Muscle Groups

Day 1: Biceps, Triceps, Quadriceps, Hamstrings

Workout one	Workout two	Workout three
Seated dumbell curls	Standing EZ curls	Cable curls
Preacher curls	Concentration curls	Prone incline curls
Triceps pressdowns	Two-arm overhead cable extensions	One-arm overhead dumbbell extensions
Overhead rope extensions	Triceps kickbacks	Triceps dips
Leg presses	Lunges	Squats
Front kicks	Sissy squats	Leg extensions
Stiff-legged deadlifts	Seated leg curls	Lying leg curls
Standing leg curls	Hyperextensions	Good mornings

Day 2: Chest, Back, Shoulders, Calves, Abs

Incline dumbbell presses	Flat machine presses	Push-ups
Pec decks	Cable crossovers	Incline flys
Front lat pulldowns	Chins	Reverse lat pulldowns
Seated rows	One-arm dumbbell rows	Dumbbell pullovers
Dumbbell shoulder presses	Arnold presses	Machine shoulder presses
Lateral raises	Bent lateral raises	Upright rows
Standing calf raises	Donkey calf raises	Toe presses
Seated calf raises	One-legged seated calf raises	Seated calf raises
Crunches	Seated rope crunches	Rope crunches
Hanging leg raises	Reverse crunches	Bench leg raises

As in the body-conditioning routine, the order in which you perform exercises is important in achieving the best results. To optimize this sequence, you should first consider which secondary muscles you will use in training each major muscle group. Then, structure your routine to rest these muscles while training the next muscle group. For instance, in the example above, you work the chest (which uses shoulders and triceps) first in the sequence. Next, you train the back (which uses biceps), allowing the triceps and shoulders to rest for a brief period and recover some strength. The arrangement is self-explanatory thereafter, providing enough recovery time for secondary muscle movers while training the target muscles wholeheartedly.

You will notice that you train the abdominals with the same frequency as every other muscle. This will be a shock to many women, who have been told that they should perform abdominal exercises daily to achieve maximum definition. This half-truth, promoted for years without supporting documentation, has somehow been taken as gospel. Because the abdominals are an endurance-oriented muscle, they might be able to bear a slightly greater tolerance for training frequency. As with all muscles, however, you must provide adequate recuperation to maximize results. As you have learned, quantity does not necessarily produce quality. Abdominals can be overtrained just like any other muscle group. Use discretion in training frequency.

Moreover, the abdominals are worked indirectly while training other muscle groups. Many fitness professionals overlook this fact. Exercises such as triceps pressdowns, lat pulldowns, squats, and others use the abdominals as supporting muscles in the performance of the movement. Training in the High-Energy Fitness system will provide substantial secondary stress to the abdominal muscles every time you work out. I have worked with many women who had trained their abdominals every day for years. After cutting the volume of their training and employing proper intensity to their efforts, they substantially improved the definition of their abdominal muscles.

Thus, I recommend that you train your abdominals as you would any other muscle group, focusing on quality, not quantity. If you do not feel you are seeing adequate results, examine your training methods before adding extra sets or training frequency. Training this area more often than a few times a week will be superfluous and can actually impair your development. Moreover, remember that if you have excess body fat in this area, you will never see the muscle that you have worked so hard to build!

In this phase of training it is generally better to work your upper body before training your legs. Your lower body will be fatigued and perhaps slightly unstable immediately after intense training. Thus, it can be difficult for your legs to support your body in many exercises performed in the standing position. This will restrict your upper-body work to seated movements. Moreover, leg training tends to be aerobic, sapping your energy resources. By training your lower body at the end of your routine, you will get more from your upper-body efforts without significantly affecting your leg workout.

Another important goal in this phase of training is creating aesthetic balance in your proportions. As previously mentioned, you should be in tune with the overall symmetry of your physique and how each muscle complements the others. In most cases, one side of your body will be stronger or better developed than the other side (your right biceps might be stronger than your left or your left hamstring might have more shape than your right, and so forth), causing asymmetrical development. Although your genes play a major role in determining symmetry, external factors can also affect your proportions. For example, women often carry their pocket books on a certain side, increasing their strength on that side at the expense of the other. Bringing both sides of your body into alignment is an important concern.

To ensure symmetrical development, you should increase the use of dumbbells and one-arm cable exercises in your routine. These movements require each side of your body to perform an equal amount of work (as opposed to barbells and machines, where your stronger side tends to compensate for your weaker side). Using these movements will balance development not only between different muscle groups but also between each side of your body. Over time, you will bring your entire body into harmony.

Finally, after training in the toning and shaping phase of this system for a time, you should begin to use supersets in your routine. A superset comprises two exercises performed consecutively, with no rest between them. Supersets will further increase workout intensity and, because of the limited rest intervals, heighten fat burning to an even greater degree.

In the scheme of this routine, each superset counts as two sets, adding to the fast pace of your workout. On average, a muscle begins to recuperate four seconds after completion of a set. Thus, in a superset, you should attempt to move from one exercise to the other within this period. Several different combinations can create an effective superset. The following are some of the better ones:

• *A particularly effective superset links a compound movement with an isolation movement.* Some examples of supersets using this premise are leg presses with leg extensions for the legs, incline presses with pec deck flys for the chest, and shoulder presses with lateral raises for the shoulders.

• *Nonweighted exercises also work well in supersets, especially for the legs.* You can train to failure on a weighted movement, then have enough energy to perform a nonweighted leg exercise for 15 repetitions. Some examples of combining weighted and nonweighted movements into supersets are leg presses with sissy squats, front squats with walking lunges, and stiff-legged deadlifts with hyper-extensions.

• *Agonist-antagonist muscle groups are another excellent combination for supersets.* Some examples are biceps with triceps (rope hammer curls with nosebreakers, incline curls with overhead rope extensions), chest with back (incline dumbbell presses with behind-the-neck lat pulldowns, flat flys with seated rows), quadri-ceps with hamstrings (hack squats with lying leg curls, front squats with reverse hyperextensions).

Unilateral (one-arm or one-leg) movements do not translate well into supersets. Exercises performed unilaterally provide too much rest for the side that is not active, thereby decreasing the benefit of a superset. Thus, exercises like concen-tration curls and one-arm dumbbell rows are poor choices for inclusion in a superset. Experiment with various combinations, trying different supersets for each muscle group. As with all facets of training, variation is a key to achieving results.

When you feel that you are ready to take the final step and undertake targeted bodysculpting, you should first consider several points. Because this is a progres-sive system, you will have to increase your effort to secure results. You should meet the following provisions before you go forward:

• *Make sure that you have mastered all the principles and concepts of this system.* The complexities of fitness should be second nature at this point. You should have a clear grasp of all training fundamentals. It is not enough to have an overview of these factors; they must be ingrained in your subconscious. Targeted body-sculpting leaves no time for learning your way.

• *Make sure that you have accomplished the objectives of this phase of training.* The toning and shaping routine is intended to create the basis on which to employ advanced bodysculpting techniques. If you are still in the rudimentary stages of developing your physique, continuing with this routine will better help you achieve long-term progress. You should not try to run before you are able to walk—doing so is bound to make you fall.

• *Make sure that you are willing and able to push yourself to the limit.* The increase in intensity and effort will be even greater than before. Targeted bodysculpting is for those who desire to maximize their body's potential. If this is your aim, you must be willing to endure the work required to reach those heights. You should be able to move through the toning and shaping routine easily, feeling both mentally and physically able to go beyond your current training pace. If you cannot do this, the advanced routine will be too intense.

If you have any doubt about whether you meet these prerequisites, continue with the toning and shaping routine until you are ready to move forward. Do not feel that there is a time limit for your progress or even that you must ever take the next step. You can acquire an excellent physique using this routine and, depending on your expectations and goals, might be content to continue with it indefinitely. But if you aspire to master your physique and reach your ultimate potential, you need to take the final step. If this is your mission, the next chapter will help you realize your dreams!

Chest Exercises

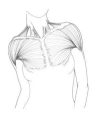

INCLINE DUMBBELL FLYS

Lie on an incline bench set at 30 to 40 degrees, planting your feet on the floor. Grasp two dumbbells and hold them to your sides, slightly bending your elbows. Your palms should be turned in and toward the ceiling, your upper arms roughly parallel with the bench. Slowly raise the weights in a circular motion, as if hugging a large tree. Gently touch the weights at the top of the move and, after feeling a contraction in your chest, return to the starting position.

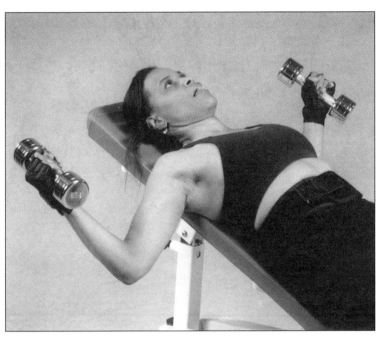

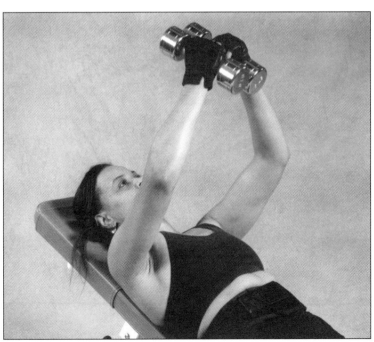

Back Exercises

CHINS

Take a shoulder-width, overhand grip on a chinning bar. Fully straighten your arms so that you feel a complete stretch in your lats. Bend your knees and cross your ankles. Keeping your back arched, slowly pull yourself up until your chin rises above the bar. Contract your lats. Slowly lower yourself to the starting position.

Shoulder Exercises

SHOULDER PRESSES

Sit at the edge of a flat bench. Grasp a barbell, your palms turned away from you, and rest the barbell on the back of your neck. Slowly press the barbell directly over your head, contracting your deltoids at the top of the move. Return to the starting position.

Shoulder Exercises

Dumbbell Shoulder Presses

Sit at the edge of a flat bench. Bring two dumbbells to shoulder level, your palms facing away from you. Slowly press the dumbbells directly up and in, touching them directly over your head. Contract your deltoids. Reverse direction, returning the dumbbells along the same arc to the start position.

Machine Shoulder Presses

Sit in a shoulder press machine. Grasp the handles with your palms facing away from you. Slowly press the handles directly upward and over your head, contracting your deltoids at the top of the move. Reverse direction, returning the handles to the start position.

Biceps Exercises

INCLINE CURLS

Lie on a 45-degree incline bench. Grasp two dumbbells with your palms facing forward and allow the weights to hang by your hips. Keeping your upper arm stable, slowly curl the dumbbells toward your shoulders. Keep your elbows back. Contract your biceps. Return to the starting position.

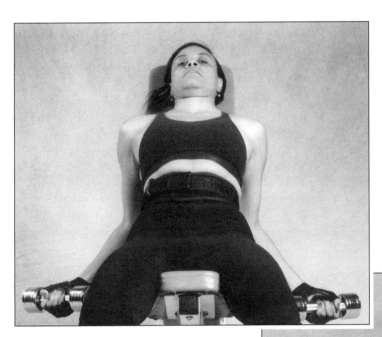

Prone Incline Curls

Follow the directions for incline curls, except lie face-down on the bench. Hold two dumbbells straight down from your shoulders. Slowly curl the dumbbells to your shoulders, keeping your upper arms stable.

Triceps Exercises

ONE-ARM OVERHEAD DUMBBELL EXTENSIONS

With your feet firmly on the floor, grasp a dumbbell in your right hand. Bend your elbow and hang the weight behind your head as far as comfortably possible. Slowly straighten your right arm, keeping your elbow back and pointed to the ceiling. Contract your right triceps. Slowly return to the starting position. Repeat with your left arm after finishing the desired reps on your right.

Triceps Exercises

TWO-ARM OVERHEAD CABLE EXTENSIONS

Turn away from a high cable pulley. With your palms turned out, grasp a straight bar attached to the pulley and bend forward. Keeping your elbows close to your ears, bend your elbows and hang your hands behind your head as far as comfortably possible. Slowly straighten your arms, keeping your elbows back. Contract your triceps. Slowly return to the starting position.

Triceps Exercises

OVERHEAD ROPE EXTENSIONS

Turn away from a high cable pulley. Bend forward and, with your palms facing each other, grasp a rope attached to the pulley. Keeping your elbows at your ears, bend your elbows and hang your hands behind your head as far as comfortably possible. Slowly straighten your arms, keeping your elbows back. Contract your triceps. Return to the starting position.

Quadriceps Exercises

FRONT KICKS

Attach a cuff to a low cable pulley and your right ankle. Face away from the pulley and grasp a sturdy portion of the machine for support. Slowly bring your foot forward and up, contracting your right quad at the top of the movement. Return to the starting position. Repeat with your left leg after finishing the desired reps on your right.

Quadriceps Exercises

SISSY SQUATS

Stand with your feet shoulder-width apart. Grasp an incline bench with one hand and rise onto your toes. In one motion, slowly slant your torso back, bend your knees, and lower your body. Thrust your knees forward as you descend and lean back until your torso is almost parallel with the floor. Return to the starting position.

Hamstring-Glute Exercises

STANDING CABLE LEG CURLS

Attach a cuff to a low cable pulley and secure the cuff to your right ankle. Face the weight stack and grasp a sturdy portion of the machine for support. Keeping your thigh perpendicular to the ground, slowly bring your right foot back and up toward your butt. Contract your right hamstring. Slowly return to the starting position. Repeat with your left leg after finishing the desired reps on your right.

Abdominal Exercises

ROPE CRUNCHES

Facing the machine, kneel in front of a high pulley. Grasp a rope attached to the pulley. Keeping your elbows close to your ears, slowly curl forward, bringing your elbows to your knees. Contract your abs. Slowly uncurl, returning to the starting position.

Seated Rope Crunches

Follow the directions for rope crunches, except sit in a lat pulldown machine with your legs secured by the restraint pads. Grasp a rope attached to the pulley. Keeping your elbows close to your ears, slowly bring your elbows to your knees.

Abdominal Exercises

CRUNCHES

See instructions and photos of crunches on page 54.

Reverse Crunches

Follow the directions for crunches, except lie on the bench. Hold the sides of the bench and bring your knees to your stomach. Lift your butt and press your upper back to the bench.

Donna Richardson: National Aerobics Champion, Star of ESPN's "Fitness Pros"

Height: 5'4"

Weight: 115

14932 Paddock Drive, Wellington, FL 33414

Photo courtesy of Donna Richardson

Donna Richardson exudes fitness. A former dancer, Donna lives and breathes exercise. She is in perpetual motion, always remaining active in one way or another. Accordingly, her fitness routine is multi-faceted and includes a wide variety of different activities.

Because of her background in dance, Donna is especially attuned to the benefits of a regimented program of stretching. "In my opinion, the biggest mistake that women make in their fitness program is not giving enough attention to flexibility training. Most women are so pressed for time that they can't be bothered with stretching and warming up. Then they wonder why they're so sore after their workout!"

To Donna, stretching is both refreshing as well as therapeutic. "Once you've incorporated stretching into your routine, you feel like a new person. In addition to relaxing your body, it also helps to relax your mind, as well. And there are many different ways to make stretching fun. You can take a dance class, perform yoga or buy a tape and stretch in the comfort of your own home. The important thing is—like they say in the commercial—just do it."

Donna feels that, through proper education, flexibility training can be brought into the mainstream. "I think it's essential to emphasize the importance of stretching, because so many people just aren't aware of the benefits that it provides. Not only does it help to prevent injuries, but it also flushes waste from your system and improves your body alignment. I firmly believe that you can't be physically fit unless you have achieved a good deal of flexibility."

And, if you don't care about the health and wellness benefits, Donna points out that stretching can even help to improve your aesthetics. "While the effects of stretching aren't as obvious as getting 'six-pack abs' or losing two inches off your waist, it does promote better posture and other subtle differences that enhance your overall appearance. That alone should be reason enough to include it in your workout."

Donna's training tip

"Take charge of your body—don't let it take charge of you! Yes, it does take time to reap the rewards from exercise, but the payback that you get for your efforts is a thousand times greater than what you put into it."

5 Targeted Bodysculpting

You must have a strong desire to rise to the challenge of sculpting your body to its ultimate potential. Training at a level that will maximize your shape and definition requires tremendous effort. The further you progress in your fitness endeavors, the more difficult it is to improve your physique. You can achieve roughly 90 percent of your potential by adhering to the toning and shaping phase of this system—the remaining 10 percent is what separates the good from the extraordinary. If you are prepared to meet this challenge, the targeted body-sculpting phase of the High-Energy Fitness system will take you all the way to physique heaven!

You should, at this point, possess a shapely, toned physique that needs only some fine tuning. Your goals are now probably lofty. Perhaps you have aspirations to become a fitness competitor, or maybe you just want to look great in a bikini. Whatever your desire, you control your destiny. You can add more shape, size, or definition to a specific muscle and focus on creating balanced, aesthetic proportions. Consider yourself a sculptor and your body an unfinished statue in need of some finishing touches. This is where bodysculpting becomes both a science and an art.

The advanced phase of this system is the essence of High-Energy Fitness—a merging of mind and muscle to achieve physical perfection. To accomplish the final phase of sculpting your physique, the routine will be split into three parts. You will perform more exercises and sets per muscle group. Because this will require more intensity and a greater volume of training, your body will necessarily need more recuperation. Thus, you will train each muscle group only once per week.

Repetitions

Use a variety of repetition ranges to achieve your fitness goals. The following rules apply to repetition ranges:

- A program using 4 to 6 repetitions is best for increasing strength and power. This repetition range, considered low, is oriented to power-lifting goals.
- A program using 8 to 12 repetitions, a moderate repetition range, is best for increasing overall muscularity. This range is oriented toward developing a bodybuilding physique.
- A program using 15 to 20 repetitions is best for increasing muscular hardness and definition. This high repetition range is oriented to achieving lean muscle tone.

Accordingly, High-Energy Fitness advocates high repetitions, with a target of 15 repetitions per set. Because our goal is toning, high repetitions will help bring about the ideal complement of muscular shape and definition without inducing considerable muscular size. Some women ask if going beyond 30 reps will produce even better muscle tone (again, the concept that more must be better). Unfortunately, no definitive study supports this thesis. It appears that you reach a point of diminishing returns when you increase repetitions to more than 20 per set. Beyond this, a woman tends to lose her concentration, reducing the effectiveness of the exercise. Hence, I recommend a target of 15 repetitions per set.

The speed with which to perform repetitions is also an area of debate. Controversy exists among fitness professionals about the best speed with which to perform a repetition. Studies conducted on this subject have been largely inconclusive. In the High-Energy Fitness system, how fast you perform a repetition is relatively unimportant as long as the weight remains under control. Make sure that your target muscle directs each repetition; allow the muscle to move the weight during both the positive and negative phases of the movement. Momentum or gravity should never dictate the speed of a repetition. Use a smooth, consistent motion to ensure complete stimulation of your target muscles and reduce the possibility of injury.

It is also beneficial to perform repetitions rhythmically. Each repetition should flow into the next, creating a distinct tempo to the set. This helps set a groove during the workout, which produces a structured training regimen. By training to a pulse, you will find it easier to concentrate throughout the set and thereby target the proper muscles.

Since there are nine categories of major muscles, you can split your routine by training three muscle groups each workout. I recommend the following combination as an effective training split:

- Day 1: Chest, back, abdominals
- Day 2: Quadriceps, hamstrings, calves
- Day 3: Shoulders, biceps, triceps

This combination works all the major muscles and allows for excellent rest and recuperation between agonist-antagonist muscle groups. Of course, alternative ways of splitting your routine can be equally effective. There is no best method for combining muscle groups into a routine. Do not be afraid to experiment with different combinations to see what works best for you.

In the targeted bodysculpting phase the system is more flexible so that you can customize the routine to your individual needs. The art of bodysculpting is specific to the individual and ultimately subject to your idea of the ideal female physique. It is sometimes difficult to see yourself as you really are, and women often have a distorted opinion of their own bodies. Therefore, you should try to look at yourself objectively, as if you were evaluating the physique of another woman. When you are in tune with your body, you can make intelligent decisions about improving your deficiencies.

Although this phase of High-Energy Fitness is dynamic, the basis of the system is nevertheless structured. Without structure, training becomes undisciplined and chaotic, ultimately leading to decreased results. The following is the protocol for targeted bodysculpting:

Objective self-evaluation brings you in tune with your body.

- *Exercises:* You should use from two to four exercises for each major muscle group, and, as always, apply as much variety to your routine as possible. At this level, you should combine the exercises to sculpt your proportions. Several exercise variables will affect your bodysculpting results, including the angle of pull in a movement, the amount of stretch involved in the exercise, the positioning of your hands or feet, and the ability to isolate and contract a specific muscle. Considering these factors, I have indexed the exercises into classes that work synergistically with one another. By combining the exercises as specified, you can maximize shape and definition in each muscle complex. You should normally choose at least one exercise from each class. But if you want to pay special heed to a certain area, feel free to do so. Also, although it is normally better to train larger muscle groups at the beginning of your workout, you should prioritize lagging muscles by training them first. In this way, you will have more energy to train those muscles and will get greater results from your efforts.

- *Sets:* You should employ anywhere from 6 to 12 sets per muscle group, using two to four different exercises each workout. Because larger muscles have a greater capacity for work, they can endure more total sets than smaller muscle groups. Moreover, smaller muscles will receive secondary stress in many exercises (the arms during most upper-body work and the hamstrings and glutes on various compound leg movements), further reducing the need for additional sets. Table 5.1 details the various muscle groups and the approximate number of sets that you can perform for each category. At the advanced level, High-Energy Fitness is intense, so I advise you to start on the lower end of the recommended set ranges. Being overzealous can lead to overtraining, which will retard your progress. As you move forward, assess your results and add additional sets as needed.

- *Rest:* As in the lower-level routines, keep rest intervals between sets to no more than 20 to 30 seconds. If definition is your aim, keep rest intervals as short you can. Supersets and giant sets (discussed on page 82) will provide an ultrahigh energy pace to your workout. Your heart rate will be significantly elevated and your breathing fairly rapid throughout the workout.

- *Repetitions:* The target repetition number will expand to 15 to 20 per set, allowing additional flexibility for toning and sculpting. You can, however, selectively use lower repetitions where appropriate. Perhaps you want to add size to a specific muscle group to bring your body into proportion. If so, use fewer reps for that particular muscle (in the range of 8 to 12 repetitions). Again, make sure to train with good form and apply continuous tension to your muscles during each repetition.

Table 5.1 Number of Sets per Muscle Group

Muscle group	Sets
Back	9 to 12
Chest	9 to 12
Shoulders	9 to 12
Triceps	8 to 10
Biceps	6 to 9
Quadriceps	9 to 12
Hamstrings and glutes	8 to 10
Calves	6 to 9
Abdominals	6 to 9

- *Intensity:* After a sufficient warm-up, you should perform all sets to momentary muscular failure (100 percent intensity). Thus, you should employ a weight that causes failure on or about the 15th repetition. Because you are resting only briefly, you will certainly have to use lighter weights on each successive set. Muscular fatigue will occur rapidly. If you feel that a certain muscle group is overdeveloped, you should train it at about 75 percent intensity. Never discontinue training a muscle, regardless of whether it is of concern to you. This will ensure that you maintain a degree of hardness and definition and avoid developing muscular imbalances due to disuse.

The element in the margin below summarizes the specific protocols for the targeted bodysculpting phase. Hundreds of women have successfully used these protocols, which have endured the test of time. Therefore, you should hesitate before deviating from the basic guidelines. As previously noted, however, this phase is dynamic. You should adapt the guidelines to your physique and abilities. Within the framework of this system, you should endeavor to turn your body into a work of art!

Using these protocols, you should now begin to employ giant sets in your workout. A giant set incorporates three or more different exercises in succession, without rest between them (as opposed to a superset, which uses two sequential movements). A superset equals two sets; a giant set counts as three (or more) sets. By performing three or more exercises consecutively, you are able to generate more intensity than you can with supersets. Because you perform the exercises in rapid succession, you will achieve a considerable aerobic effect, promoting accelerated fat-burning capacity. Giant sets are thus particularly effective for maximizing definition and muscle tone.

To get the most out of a giant set, it is best to choose exercises that require alternative angles or different muscular actions in the performance of the movement. For example, an excellent combination for a giant set of the quadriceps could include squats, leg

Bodysculpting Protocols

Number of exercises:	2 to 4 per muscle group
Number of sets:	2 to 3 per exercise
Rest between sets:	20 to 30 seconds
Repetitions per set:	15 to 20 per set (as low as 8 for selected muscle groups)
% of maximum weight	Failure on all sets (75% for selected muscle groups)

extensions, and walking lunges. Squats stimulate the entire quadriceps as well as the hamstrings and glutes, leg extensions isolate the lower portion of the quadriceps, and walking lunges stress alternative fibers of the quadriceps while providing a considerable aerobic benefit. Although these movements all stress the quadriceps, they complement each other to produce a sum greater than their parts.

Again, you should pay heed to the order of the movements, which is important for optimal exercise performance. Squats are a compound movement that stresses all the muscles of the upper leg. Because squats require the most effort, perform them first in the sequence to allow for maximal strength and energy. Do leg extensions second to isolate the quadriceps. Because this is a seated, single-joint movement, energy reserves are not as much of a concern and you should be able to push through the set. Finally, walking lunges are a nonweighted movement that is a great finishing exercise. It will elevate your heart rate and, although it is a compound movement, will work many of the muscle fibers that were neglected in the squat.

To apply advanced bodysculpting techniques correctly, you must cultivate a working knowledge of your individual muscles. In the beginning stages of High-Energy Fitness, when your bodysculpting capabilities were limited, it was enough to have merely a general grasp of this information. To take your physique to the next level, however, you should now understand how each muscle affects your proportions. I recommend that you look over the anatomical diagrams in chapter 1 (see pages 6 and 7) and study the composition and proximity of the various muscles.

Before constructing the specifics of your routine, you should assess your physique to choose a course of action. Although you cannot change your God-given genetics, you have substantial control over the shape of your physique. Bodysculpting gives you the ability to alter your proportions significantly, creating a balanced, symmetrical body. For instance, if you have a naturally blocky waist, there is no way to change this fact (short of radical surgery). Although you can reduce fat to maintain hardness in this area, your waist will still have a blocky appearance. However, by employing bodysculpting techniques and adding muscle to your medial deltoid and upper back areas, you will increase your shoulder-to-waist differential. This will give you the illusion of having a smaller waist, creating an hourglass physique. Bodysculpting is all about creating illusion. With knowledge and effort you can mask your genetic limitations.

In subsequent chapters, I will discuss each of the nine major muscle groups and examine the possibilities of each for adding shape and definition. Exercises will be classified into groups that

Bodysculpting techinques can create the illusion of a slim waist.

will show you how to combine movements for maximal effect. State-of-the-art training tips will explain how to optimize performance. Finally, I will present sample routines that illustrate the possibilities for creating an exciting, custom-designed routine.

Of course, make sure to warm up thoroughly before each workout. The warm-up outlined in chapter 2 is still sufficient, regardless of your level of expertise. You may, however, want to perform a few light sets of an exercise for the muscles that you will be training. This safeguard will help supply your muscles with ample blood flow, preparing them for the intense training required at this level.

6 Sexy Chest

Virtually every woman covets a pert, shapely chest. Unfortunately, breast tissue will often head south as you grow older, succumbing to the effects of gravity, pregnancy, and age. "How can I prevent my breasts from sagging?" is one of the most common questions I am asked.

Although training your chest will not change the overall structure of your breasts (breast tissue is fat and, as previously discussed, you cannot shape fat), it can help to prevent them from drooping by firming the surrounding muscles of the breastbone. By toning these muscles, you can provide a distinct lift to your breasts, helping to offset the ravages of time.

Moreover, although it won't beef up your bustline, training can create the illusion of a fuller, sexier chest. Rather than seeking a surgical solution to pump up your assets, you can train to secure a natural edge. For instance, you can develop your inner chest to suggest more cleavage, or you can work your upper chest to make your breasts appear more ample. As the sculptor, you have the power to shape this area any way you choose.

The chest is a unique structure. It has attachments at three different bones—the breast bone (sternum), collar bone (clavicle), and upper arm (humerus)—and its muscle fibers run in many directions. Hence, the chest can benefit from exercises that use a variety of angles as well as movements that provide a different stretch and contraction. Accordingly, exercises for the chest will be classified into compound and isolation movements. Additional attention will be given to a movement's ability to stretch and contract the muscles of the chest.

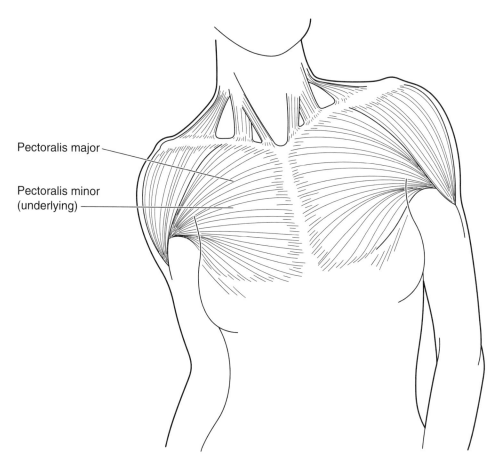

Muscles of the chest.

- *Class one—presses, push-ups, and chest dips.* These compound movements stress the overall pec as well as many secondary muscles. They help to give overall fullness to this area and provide stability to the muscle fibers surrounding the sternum (the part that attaches to the breasts, giving them support). By varying the angles, you can shift the emphasis of the movement to the upper, mid, or lower portions of the chest.

- *Class two—dumbbell flys.* These isolation movements primarily work the chest on a horizontal plane. Because of gravitational pull, they exert great force at the beginning portion of the move. As you bring the weight up, however, the stress gradually diminishes to the point where muscular tension is virtually non-existent at the finish position. Thus, in order to maximize results, it is imperative to focus on the first half of each rep, making sure to get a complete stretch at the bottom. But don't allow your arms to stretch significantly below parallel with the floor. Doing so places undue stress on the shoulder joint and can lead to serious injury.

- *Class three—pec deck flys and crossovers.* These isolation movements help to give a polished look to the pectoral region. Because these movements allow continuous tension to be provided, an intense contraction can be achieved at the finish position. Hence, by forcefully squeezing your pecs together at peak contraction, you can recruit muscle fibers that are impossible to activate in free weight exercises.

Angles

A muscle is made up of thousands of tiny fibers. When properly executed, a weighted exercise will target specific fibers within a muscle or group of muscles. Each exercise, however, will hit only a portion of the fibers in these muscles. Although certain exercises stimulate a greater number of muscle fibers than others, it is beneficial to use a variety of exercises that work a muscle from different angles. Using different exercise angles will stress all the fibers in a muscle. This will help refine each muscle completely and develop overall aesthetic symmetry in your physique.

After you become experienced at training, you might decide to use certain exercise angles more frequently to accentuate lagging muscle groups. You can, for instance, choose exercises that focus on the upper chest, side deltoid, or virtually any muscle. This can aid the bodysculpting process by helping to bring individual muscles into proportion with one other. But realize that this is not an exact process. Although an exercise can exert more stress on specific fibers within a muscle, it will commonly involve other areas of the same muscle to some degree (and perhaps secondary muscles too). Thus, you will reach a limit to how much muscular isolation you can achieve with this technique. Moreover, regardless of your level of training expertise, you should always incorporate in your routine exercises that encompass different angles to guarantee complete, symmetrical development of all muscle groups.

Bodysculpting Tips

1. The three basic angles that you can use in chest training (incline, flat, and decline) emphasize different portions of the pecs. An incline exercise accentuates the upper chest, flat works the middle portion of the chest, and decline stresses the lower region. By assessing the symmetry of your chest, you can selectively use these angles to augment your proportions.

2. The upper chest is perhaps the most important area to develop, making incline exercises highly beneficial. The upper region of your chest encompasses most of the shape in this area and gives the appearance of a firm, elevated chest. It is best to keep the angle on incline exercises between 30 and 40 degrees. Using a steeper angle activates the frontal portion of the deltoids, taking much of the stress away from the chest muscles.

3. The lower chest is one of the easiest portions to develop and usually needs little stimulation. Further, a woman's anatomical structure makes developing this area of limited utility. Thus, unless the lower portion of the chest is a specific weak spot, use decline exercises sparingly, mostly for variety.

4. Push-ups can be a great complementary exercise, especially when combined with other exercises in a superset or giant set. Depending on your body weight, you may find these exercises difficult to execute. If you have trouble performing "military" push-ups, start by using the modified position (from your knees). Gradually attempt to perform the exercise military style until you can perform a full set.

TARGETED WORKOUTS FOR THE CHEST

WORKOUT	EXERCISE	SETS
1	Incline dumbbell presses (p. 30)	2
	Flat bench flys (p. 34) supersetted with push-ups (p. 32)	2
	Pec deck flys (p. 33)	3

WORKOUT	EXERCISE	SETS
2	Incline machine chest presses (p. 31) supersetted with incline dumbbell flys (p. 65) and cable crossovers (p. 90)	3

WORKOUT	EXERCISE	SETS
3	Chest dips (p. 89)	2
	Incline dumbbell presses (p. 30)	2
	Flat bench flys (p. 34)	3
	One-arm cable crossovers (p. 91)	3

WORKOUT	EXERCISE	SETS
4	Incline machine chest presses (p. 31) supersetted with incline dumbbell flys (p. 65)	3
	Low cable crossovers (p. 91)	3
	Pec deck flys (p. 33)	3

Chest Exercises

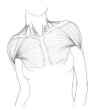

CHEST DIPS

Grasp the bars on a parallel bar apparatus with your palms turned in. Bend your legs to a 90-degree angle, cross your ankles, and tilt your upper body forward with your hips to the back. Maintaining a distinct forward tilt, slowly bend your elbows and lower your body as far as comfortably possible. Return to the starting position.

Chest Exercises

CABLE CROSSOVERS

Grasp the handles of an overhead pulley (cable crossover machine). Stand with your left foot about 12 inches behind your right foot and slightly bend forward at the waist. Slowly pull the handles down and across your body in a semicircle. Bring your hands together at hip level and squeeze your chest so that you feel a contraction. Slowly reverse direction, returning to the starting position.

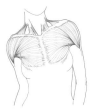

Chest Exercises

One-Arm Cable Crossovers

Grasp the handle of an overhead pulley (cable crossover machine) with your left hand. Stand with your feet about shoulder-width apart and your torso bent slightly forward at the waist. Slowly pull the handle down and across your body in a semicircle. When your hand crosses the midline of your body, squeeze your chest muscles so that you feel a contraction. Reverse direction, returning to the starting position. Repeat with your right arm after performing the desired number of reps on your left.

Low Cable Crossovers

Grasp the loop handles of a low pulley (cable crossover machine). Stand with your feet about shoulder-width apart and bend slightly forward at the waist. Slowly pull both handles down and across your body in a semicircle. Bring your hands together at hip level and squeeze your chest muscles so that you feel a contraction. Reverse direction, returning to the starting position.

Susie Curry: Women's World Pro Fitness Champion

Height: 5'2"

Weight: 115

P.O. Box 293, Presto, PA 15142-0293

Photo © J.M. Manion/J.M. Productions

Susie Curry is regarded as one of the most defined women on the fitness scene. She is noted for her sleek muscularity and hard muscle tone. In order to achieve her amazing condition, Susie endures a grueling pre-contest regimen. Starting approximately 12 weeks before a competition, she completely restructures both her training and nutritional schedules.

During the pre-contest period, Susie adjusts her diet so that she is eating more protein and fewer carbohydrates. "I eat a lot of egg whites and chicken breasts, which helps to get me lean and reduces water retention," she states. "I make sure not to go too low on my carbs, though. Carbs are my main source of energy and if I'm totally carb-depleted, I don't have the stamina to make it through my routine."

Furthermore, Susie relies heavily on protein shakes to supplement her nutritional scheme. "It's difficult to take in clean, quality nutrients from regular food alone. Protein shakes are really convenient and easy to prepare. They're very low in fat and sugar, and provide a great source of protein."

In respect to her training, Susie splits her routine into three separate sessions per day. This way, she is able to recoup her energy so that she is fresh every time she trains. "In the last few weeks before a show, my entire weight training routine is basically one big superset. I go from one exercise to another with virtually no rest in between sets."

In addition, as a means to increase muscular endurance, Susie utilizes very high reps, especially when training her lower body. "For my leg routine, I'll go as high as 25 to 50 reps. By this time, I've already added the necessary shape to my muscles so my focus is on bringing out the last bit of detail."

Although she adheres to a fitness-oriented lifestyle year round, Susie acknowledges that subtle changes in training and nutrition can be paramount to looking your absolute best. "My weight really doesn't fluctuate that much throughout the year—maybe five pounds or so. But when you're talking about looking good versus looking great, those few extra pounds can make a huge difference."

Susie's training tip

"See a goal, set the goal, and work hard toward achieving the goal. There is no miracle to being fit or staying in shape—it's all hard work."

7 Hourglass Back

The back is a muscle group that women often neglect. Because you do not readily see these muscles when looking in a mirror, you may leave them out of your training regimen in favor of more showy muscles. A well-sculpted back, however, in conjunction with the shoulders, can help to create the illusion of a small waist. This will produce feminine body lines that help to accentuate an hourglass physique. Furthermore, although you may have difficulty seeing these muscles, bringing out their detail will make you look great in everything from a backless dress to a swimsuit.

The muscles of your back also play a central role in maintaining good posture. Poor posture causes you to slouch, contributing to a tired, haggard appearance. This affects how others perceive you, making you look older than your years. Conversely, when your posture is erect, you project youthful exuberance. Inevitably, you'll display an aura of self-confidence in both your professional and social endeavors.

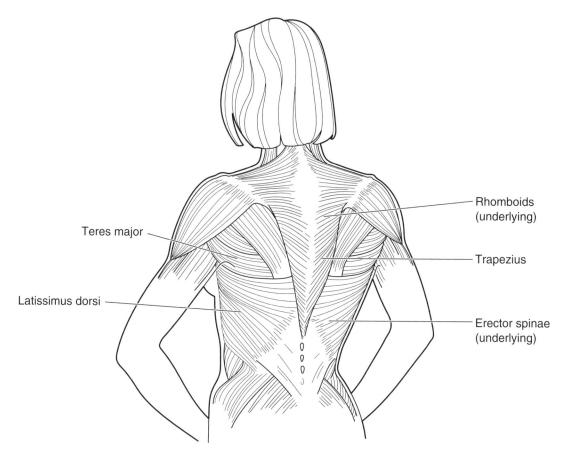

Muscles of the back.

Spot Training

It is important to train every muscle in your body at least once a week. Do not neglect any muscle group, especially in the beginning phase of your training program. Many women want to focus on trouble areas at the exclusion of training the rest of their bodies. I am often asked, "Why do I need to train my back? I don't care about my back!" The body functions holistically and muscle groups interrelate in a synergistic fashion. Ignoring certain muscle groups will disrupt the symmetry of your body and impair the aesthetics of your physique. Because muscles interact in an agonist-antagonist manner, training one muscle at the exclusion of another will create a muscular imbalance in your physique. This will alter your muscular function and make you considerably more prone to injury.

Bodysculpting Routine

The back, consisting of many individual muscles, is the largest muscle group in the upper body. Unfortunately, because of their proximity, it is virtually impossible to isolate the individual muscles. By varying the angle of pull in the exercises, however, you can stimulate most of the fibers in the various muscles of the back. Therefore, exercises for the back will be classified by the angles available in exercise performance. You can apply three separate angles of pull to produce optimal shape in this area. For best results, incorporate one from each class into every workout.

• *Class one—pulldowns and chins.* These exercises use an overhead angle that pulls in a line parallel to your body. You can create additional angles by using a straight line of pull (behind-the-neck exercises) or a frontal line of pull (leaning slightly back during performance).

• *Class two—rows.* These exercises employ a perpendicular line of pull and allow you to exert maximum contraction of the scapula (shaping many of the muscles of the inner back). They also permit you to use many one-arm movements with dumbbells and cables, helping to improve your muscular balance and symmetry.

• *Class three—straight-arm pulldowns and pullovers.* These exercises use an arcing motion, thereby activating many of the tie-in muscles between the back and chest (serratus, intercostals, and so on). Although often neglected, these exercises are an excellent complement to rows and chins and add another dimension to a well-constructed back routine.

Bodysculpting Tips

1. You should vary your hand spacing between narrow, medium, and wide grips. This will allow you to work the muscles of the back in line with the direction of the fibers of the individual muscles. Do not go more than several inches past a shoulder-width grip on any lat exercise. This will decrease the stretch to the muscle, limiting your range of motion and reducing the effectiveness of the movement.

2. Using a reverse grip on your exercises will activate the biceps to a greater degree, thereby reducing stress to the muscles of your back. Many women gravitate to these exercises because the secondary influence of the biceps makes them easier to perform. The biceps, however, are much weaker than the back and will fatigue before you fully stimulate the target muscles. Thus, you will not receive optimal benefit from the exercise. If this problem occurs, it can be helpful to use lifting straps when performing movements with a reverse grip. Otherwise, stick to a pronated (palms facing away) or neutral (palms facing one another) grip. Use the reverse grip sparingly, mostly for variety.

3. The best way to achieve definition of your inner back is by squeezing your shoulder blades (scapula) together. To bring out the detail in these muscles, you should focus on compressing your scapula toward the middle of your back on each contraction. Because the back muscles are so close together, you will usually find it difficult to acquire a mind-to-muscle link in this area. Concentrate on this squeeze to improve your results.

4. It is imperative that you achieve a full stretch on the negative portion of each repetition. Women often shorten the range of motion on back movements, focusing only on the contraction. The stretch, however, lengthens the muscles of the back, which increases both muscular stimulation and upper-body flexibility. Thus, allow the weight to pull slightly on your scapula until you feel a deep stretch in the muscles you are training.

TARGETED WORKOUTS FOR THE BACK

WORKOUT	EXERCISE	SETS
1	Front lat pulldowns (p. 101) supersetted with seated rows (p. 35)	3
	One-arm dumbbell rows (p. 37)	2
	Dumbbell pullovers (p. 98)	3

WORKOUT	EXERCISE	SETS
2	Chins (p. 66)	3
	One-arm seated rows (p. 36)	3
	Straight-arm pulldowns (p. 97)	3

WORKOUT	EXERCISE	SETS
3	Behind-the-neck lat pulldowns (p. 102)	3
	One-arm seated rows (p. 36)	4
	Dumbbell pullovers (p. 98)	3

WORKOUT	EXERCISE	SETS
4	Reverse lat pulldowns (p. 102) supersetted with T-bar rows (p. 99)	3
	One-arm standing low rows (p. 100)	3
	Straight-arm pulldowns (p. 97)	3

Back Exercises

STRAIGHT-ARM PULLDOWNS

Using an overhand grip, grasp a straight bar attached to a high pulley. Slightly bend your elbows and bring the bar to eye level. Keeping a forward tilt to your upper body, slowly pull the bar down in a semicircle until it touches your upper thighs. Contract your lats. Reverse direction, returning the bar to the starting position.

Back Exercises

DUMBBELL PULLOVERS

Lie on a flat bench. Grasp a dumbbell with both hands and raise it directly over your face. Keeping your arms slightly bent, slowly lower the dumbbell behind your head as far as comfortably possible, feeling a complete stretch in your lats. Reverse direction, squeezing your lats as you return to the starting position.

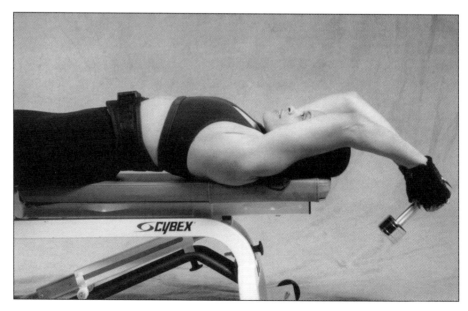

Back Exercises

T-BAR ROWS

Stand with your body bent forward and your lower back arched. Grasp the bar and hang your arms straight down from your shoulders with your palms turned toward you. Keeping your elbows close to your sides, pull the bar up as high as possible. Contract the muscles in your upper back. Return to the starting position.

Back Exercises

ONE-ARM STANDING LOW ROWS

Grasp the loop of a low pulley with your right hand. Step back from the machine and straighten your right arm so you feel a stretch in your right lat. Keep your right leg back and bend your left leg so your weight is forward. Slowly pull the loop toward your right side, keeping your elbow close. Contract your right lat. Reverse direction, returning to the starting position. Repeat with your left arm after finishing the desired reps on your right.

Back Exercises

FRONT LAT PULLDOWNS

With your hands shoulder-width apart and palms turned forward, grip a lat pulldown bar. Secure your knees under the restraint pad and fully straighten your arms so you feel a complete stretch in your lats. Maintain a slight backward tilt and arch your lower back through the move. Slowly pull the bar to your upper chest, bringing your elbows back. Squeeze your shoulder blades together. Slowly reverse direction, returning to the starting position.

Back Exercises

FRONT LAT PULLDOWNS *(continued)*

Reverse Lat Pulldowns

Grip a lat pulldown bar with your hands shoulder-width apart and your palms turned toward you. Secure your knees under the restraint pad and fully straighten your arms so you feel a complete stretch in your lats. Maintain a slight backward tilt to your body and arch your lower back through the move. Slowly pull the bar to your upper chest, bringing your elbows back as you pull. Squeeze your shoulder blades together. Reverse direction, allowing the bar to return to the starting position.

Behind-the-Neck Lat Pulldowns

With your hands shoulder-width apart and your palms turned forward, grip a lat pulldown bar. Secure your knees under the restraint pad and fully straighten your arms so you feel a complete stretch in your lats. Slowly pull the bar down behind your neck, bringing your elbows back as you pull. Squeeze your shoulder blades together. Reverse direction, returning the bar to the starting position.

8 Shapely Shoulders

The shoulders are a beautiful muscle structure that, when properly developed, can literally redefine your body. The importance of nicely rounded shoulders is clearly evident in the women's clothing industry. Most of today's leading fashion designers incorporate shoulder pads into their garments to accentuate the shoulder-to-waist differential. This creates the classic hourglass figure admired throughout the ages.

Poorly developed shoulders cannot be concealed when you wear a strapless dress or bikini. Shoulders are prominent in a variety of fashions and impact the way clothing hangs on your body. Fortunately, through targeted bodysculpting, you can acquire a natural V-taper that heightens a shapely, curvaceous physique without artificial padding. After sculpting these muscles to perfection, it won't matter what outfit you wear—you'll look great in them all.

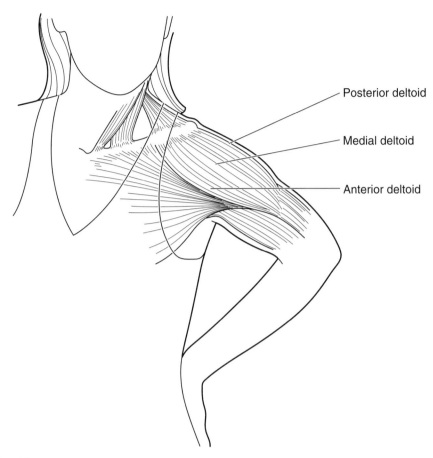

Posterior deltoid

Medial deltoid

Anterior deltoid

Muscles of the shoulder.

Bodysculpting Routine

The deltoids consist of three distinct "heads" (front, side, and rear), whose fibers run in different directions. To develop the shoulders optimally, your routine should include at least one exercise for each head of the deltoid. Hence, the exercises for shoulders will be classified by the stress applied to the deltoid head.

• *Class one—overhead presses and front raises.* Overhead presses, like all compound movements, stress many of the supporting muscles of the shoulder as well as the shoulder itself. Because the shoulders have tie-in muscles with the chest and arms, stimulating these supporting muscles helps create a polished look to your upper body. Presses tend to target the frontal deltoid, with secondary stress on the side and rear portions. Front raises are isolation movements that specifically target the front deltoid apart from the other muscles of the shoulder.

• *Class two—lateral raises and upright rows.* These exercises all emphasize the side portion of the deltoid, which creates the "cap" on your shoulders (eliminating the need for shoulder pads). This increases your shoulder-to-waist differential, which, in turn, creates the illusion of having a smaller waist. Lateral raises are isolation movements that allow you to train the side deltoid in relative exclusion to the other shoulder muscles—they are arguably the most important overall exercise for the deltoids. Upright rows, besides stressing the side deltoid, will activate supporting muscles of the upper back and shoulders. They are a good choice for adding variety to your routine.

• *Class three—posterior delt exercises.* The rear deltoid is perhaps the most difficult shoulder muscle to develop. It receives little secondary stress from other exercises and therefore needs direct stimulation through isolation movements. Ignoring this muscle will cause a structural imbalance in your deltoids, which can lead to serious injury. Exercises for the posterior delt such as rear laterals or reverse pec flys can effectively isolate this area, adding shape and symmetry to your physique.

Bodysculpting Tips

1. The front deltoid receives a great deal of stress in most chest movements and therefore can overshadow the other muscles of your shoulders. Consequently, use isolation movements for the front deltoid (for example, front raises) sparingly to avoid overdeveloping this muscle at the expense of the side and rear heads.

2. Arnold presses are a little-used exercise that can add variety to your workout and improve overall shape. They help stimulate additional muscle fibers (due to shoulder-joint rotation) neglected by other pressing movements. Used judiciously, they can provide an effective complement to standard shoulder presses.

3. Shoulder width is dictated mainly by the development of the side head of the deltoid. If you have a naturally blocky waist, you should concentrate on shaping this area to produce fullness. This will have the effect of making your waist look smaller, thus producing a more curvaceous appearance. Alternatively, if you are naturally broad shouldered or wasp waisted, you may want to reduce training intensity to the side deltoid and focus simply on maintaining hardness.

4. Shoulder injuries are common due to poor warm-up and training technique. Because the shoulder joint is highly mobile (it is the only joint that can move freely in any direction), it is more fragile and unstable than other joints. The potential for damage to this area is high. Thus, you should take extra care in warming up the shoulder girdle and use precise form in exercise performance.

TARGETED WORKOUTS FOR THE SHOULDERS

WORKOUT	EXERCISE	SETS
1	Arnold presses (p. 39)	3
	Front dumbbell raises (p. 107) supersetted with machine lateral raises (p. 109)	2
	Bent lateral raises (p. 110)	3

WORKOUT	EXERCISE	SETS
2	Shoulder presses (p. 67) supersetted with lateral raises (p. 108)	3
	Cable bent lateral raises (p. 110)	3

WORKOUT	EXERCISE	SETS
3	Machine shoulder presses (p. 68)	3
	Cable lateral raises (p. 108)	2
	Upright rows (p. 40)	2
	Bent lateral raises (p. 110)	3

WORKOUT	EXERCISE	SETS
4	Military presses (p. 38) supersetted with machine lateral raises (p. 109) and cable bent lateral raises (p. 110)	3

Shoulder Exercises

FRONT DUMBBELL RAISES

Grasp two dumbbells and allow them to hang by your hips. With a slight bend to your elbows, slowly raise the dumbbells directly in front of your body to shoulder level. Contract your delts at the top of the movement. Slowly return to the starting position.

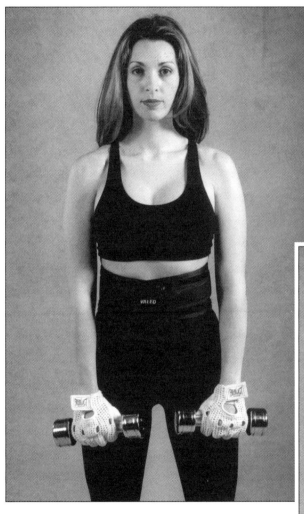

Shoulder Exercises

LATERAL RAISES

Grasp two dumbbells and allow them to hang by your hips with your palms turned toward each other. With your elbows slightly bent, raise the dumbbells up and to the sides to shoulder level. At the top of the movement, the back of the dumbbells should be slightly higher than the front. Return to the starting position.

Cable Lateral Raises

Follow the directions for lateral raises, except use a loop attachment on a low pulley and start with your right arm. Repeat with your left arm after finishing the desired reps on your right.

Shoulder Exercises

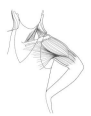

MACHINE LATERAL RAISES

Sit in a lateral raise machine. Place your forearms under the arm pads and slowly raise your elbows toward shoulder level. Contract your delts. Reverse direction, returning to the starting position.

Shoulder Exercises

BENT LATERAL RAISES

Plant your feet shoulder-width apart and grasp two dumbbells with your palms turned toward each other. Bend forward until your torso is almost parallel with the ground and hang the dumbbells in front of you. With your elbows slightly bent, raise the dumbbells up and to the sides until they are parallel with the ground. Contract your delts at the top of the movement. Slowly return to the starting position.

Cable Bent Lateral Raises

Follow the directions for bent lateral raises, except use a loop attachment on a low pulley and begin with your right hand. Repeat with your left arm after finishing the desired reps on your right.

9 Beautiful Biceps

The biceps are traditionally the most glorified of the show muscles. Shapely biceps are a symbol of fitness and strength, apparent whenever you flex your upper arm. In combination with the triceps, they produce an eye-catching appearance to your arms and make you look great in any sleeveless outfit.

The biceps also are essential in carrying out many of life's daily chores. You use your biceps in almost every lifting action, whether you are picking up your kids, putting groceries in your car, or rearranging your furniture. By strengthening this muscle group, you will be able to perform these tasks more easily and improve your overall quality of life.

Bodysculpting Routine

The biceps are a two-headed muscle on the top portion of your upper arm. Most women do not store significant body fat in this area (as opposed to the triceps, where fat is readily deposited). Thus, because the biceps are unobscured by body fat, you will often see development here more easily than you will in other muscles. Three basic positions allow you to shape your biceps: one, holding your elbows in front of your body; two, holding your elbows at the side; and three, holding your elbows behind your body. Accordingly, exercises for the biceps are classified by the amount of stretch applied to the heads of the muscle.

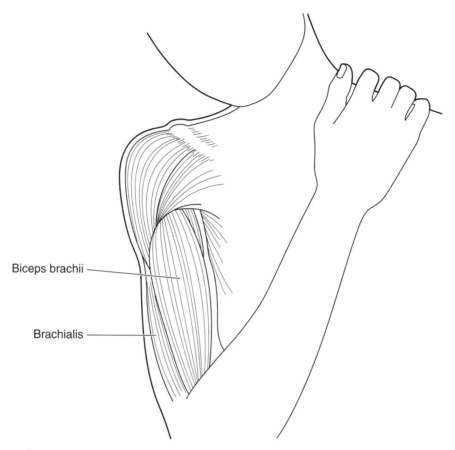

Biceps brachii

Brachialis

Muscles of the arm: biceps.

Bulking Up

Weight training can sculpt the body many different ways. You can structure a weight-training routine to add mass, increase strength, improve definition, or do virtually anything else. Contrary to popular opinion, a woman will find it extremely difficult to add a significant amount of muscle. (Many men will have the same difficulty.) Nearly all women, perhaps 99 percent, do not have the capacity to become extremely muscular because of low testosterone and limited muscle stores.

Moreover, although it can take years to develop a muscular physique, it is relatively easy to reduce muscle mass. Simply taking time off from training or reducing intensity will result in muscular atrophy. Worrying that you will get too big or muscular from training should be the least of your concerns.

• *Class one—incline curls and spider curls.* These movements stretch the long head, which sits on the outer portion of your upper arm. The long head adds fullness and helps produce a line of demarcation between the biceps and triceps.

• *Class two—preacher curls, concentration curls, and prone incline curls.* These movements limit the stretch to the long head, thereby emphasizing the short head. This area of the biceps resides on the inner portion of your upper arm and creates the biceps peak, giving the muscle a rounded appearance.

• *Class three—seated curls and standing curls.* These are combination movements that apply fairly equal stress to all aspects of the biceps. Complete stimulation is distributed through the entire muscle complex.

Bodysculpting Tips

1. You can vary your grips to emphasize different aspects of the upper arm. Three types of grips can influence muscular stress—supinated (palms facing toward your body), neutral (palms facing each other), and pronated (palms facing away from your body). Exercises using a supinated grip will shift the emphasis to the overall biceps. Exercises that use a neutral grip (that is, hammer curls) will tend to work the biceps and brachialis in tandem. Exercises that use a pronated grip will provide a great deal of stress to the forearms (this is generally not an area of concern to most women, so use these exercises sparingly).

2. It is often beneficial to use an EZ-curl bar, rather than a straight bar, when performing barbell exercises. The EZ-curl bar is curved to allow a natural tilt to the wrist. This can help alleviate pressure on the wrist and forearm muscles, a common weak spot for women, making these exercises more comfortable to execute.

3. The brachialis is a complementary muscle of the biceps that is involved in virtually all biceps movements. This muscle sits between your biceps and triceps and helps give detail to your upper arm. Moreover, when properly developed, it helps to delineate the contour of your biceps and triceps, producing a well-defined line between the two. You can best develop the brachialis by using a neutral grip (palms facing one another), making variations of the hammer curl the exercises of choice for this muscle.

4. The biceps are active in exercises for the back, receiving indirect stress in virtually all back-related movements. Moreover, they are a relatively small muscle complex, requiring limited training volume for maximal stimulation. You must use caution in working these muscles to avoid overtraining. If you find your biceps are not responding the way you would like, reduce the overall training volume or frequency, allowing more time for recuperation.

5. Genes determine the length of your biceps. If you have a short biceps muscle and a long biceps tendon, there is little you can do to lengthen the muscle (sorry, but that's the way it is). By adequately shaping this area, however, you can offset a short biceps muscle and give the illusion of fullness in the lower region, where the muscle tapers off.

TARGETED WORKOUTS FOR THE BICEPS

WORKOUT	EXERCISE	SETS
1	Incline curls (p. 69) supersetted with prone incline curls (p. 69)	2
	Standing EZ curls (p. 116)	3

WORKOUT	EXERCISE	SETS
2	Hammer curls (p. 115)	3
	One-arm dumbbell preacher curls (p. 118)	3

WORKOUT	EXERCISE	SETS
3	21s (with EZ-curl bar) (p. 117)	3
	Cable curls (p. 42)	3
	Concentration curls (p. 43)	2

WORKOUT	EXERCISE	SETS
4	Seated dumbbell curls (p. 41) supersetted with preacher curls (p. 118) and hammer curls (p. 115)	2

Biceps Exercises

HAMMER CURLS

Sit at the edge of a flat bench with your feet planted on the floor. Grasp a pair of dumbbells and hang them at your sides with your palms turned toward each other. Press your elbows to your sides, keeping them stable through the move. Slowly curl the dumbbells to your shoulders and contract your biceps at the top of the move. Return to the starting position.

Biceps Exercises

STANDING EZ CURLS

With your hands shoulder-width apart and your palms turned up, grasp an EZ-curl bar. Slightly bend and press your elbows to your sides, keeping them stable through the move. Slowly curl the bar to your shoulders and contract your biceps at the top of the move. Return to the starting position.

Biceps Exercises

21S (WITH EZ-CURL BAR)

With your hands shoulder-width apart and your palms up, grasp an EZ-curl bar. Slightly bend your knees and press your elbows to your sides, keeping them stable through the move. Slowly curl the bar until your elbows are at a 90-degree angle. Return to the starting position. After performing seven reps, curl the bar to a 90-degree angle then slowly curl the weight to your shoulders. Return to the 90-degree angle and perform seven reps. Finally, lower the bar fully and perform seven complete reps, bringing the weight to shoulder level and returning to a fully stretched position.

Biceps Exercises

PREACHER CURLS

Grasp an EZ-curl bar and place your upper arms on top of the pad of a preacher bench. Keeping your upper arms stationary, slowly curl the bar toward your shoulders. Contract your biceps at the top of the move. Reverse direction, returning to the starting position.

One-Arm Dumbbell Preacher Curls

Follow the directions for preacher curls, except use one dumbbell and begin with your right arm. Repeat with your left arm after finishing the desired reps on your right.

10 Toned Triceps

Poorly developed triceps muscles are an obvious sign of aging. Because a woman's body tends to store body fat in this area, it is one of the biggest problem spots on the female physique. When you leave this area untrained, your triceps atrophy and you eventually develop "bat wings"—loose, flabby, hanging skin. This not a pretty sight for those who want to look fit.

Furthermore, the triceps are heavily involved in many exercises for your chest and shoulders. When your triceps are weak, performing these movements can be difficult or impossible. This reduces your training capacity and ultimately your ability to redefine your body.

Fortunately, the triceps respond rapidly to training. Once you reduce body-fat levels, targeted bodysculpting will give the back of your arms a taut, toned appearance. In short order, you'll want to go sleeveless year-round.

Bodysculpting Routine

The triceps are a three-headed muscle that resides on the bottom and middle portions of the arm, comprising roughly two-thirds of the mass in this area. Because the triceps affect only a single joint (elbow), total isolation of the individual heads is not possible. This, of course, will somewhat limit your bodysculpting capability. But by varying the stretch applied to this area, you can shift the emphasis to the various heads of the muscle. Therefore, exercises for the triceps will be classified into the two basic positions that can shift stress to the different heads.

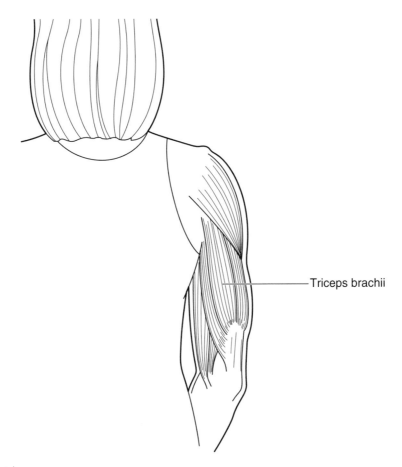

Muscles of the arm: triceps.

• *Class one—overhead extensions.* When you extend the upper arm overhead in the fully stretched position, the long head of the triceps is involved to a maximal extent. This is the part of the triceps that sits on the bottom of your arm, the place that most women complain is flabby (if your arms jiggle in the wind, you need to develop this area!). Overhead exercises for the triceps are the best way to counteract sagging arms.

• *Class two—kickbacks, pushdowns, dips, and close-grip bench.* When you keep the upper arm close to the body, you substantially reduce the stretch in the long head of the triceps. Thus, the medial and lateral heads of your triceps (the part of the triceps on the upper arm's middle portion that forms a tail) receive a greater degree of muscular stimulation. Toning this area adds detail and hardness to the upper arm, an indication of superb feminine conditioning.

Bodysculpting Tips

1. A midstretch position is essentially a compromise between the two basic triceps positions. This position places the elbows at the midway point, where your elbows are at a 90-degree angle with your body. Exercises such as nosebreakers use this modified position, which places roughly equal stress on all three heads of the triceps. These movements reduce your ability to direct stress to the various heads of the triceps, good for providing variation in your workout but somewhat limited for bodysculpting purposes.

2. As stated above, the triceps receive secondary stimulation in many shoulder and chest exercises, especially in the lower portion (long head). They are strongly involved in all presses, as well as other pushing movements. Thus, like the biceps, they are highly susceptible to overtraining. Although the triceps are a larger muscle complex than the biceps and thus can tolerate a greater volume of training, you should still be sensitive to the amount of work that you give this area. Keep the number of sets to a minimum.

3. Using a rope for triceps pressdowns can help isolate the lateral head of the muscle. Although the long head of your triceps receives secondary stress from many pressing exercises for the chest and shoulders, the lateral head receives less stimulation. Rope pressdowns use a wrist position that increases stress on the lateral head, helping to bring out greater detail in the middle portion of your arm. You can apply further stress to this area by turning your wrists at the end of the movement (so the backs of your hands face one another on the contraction). This subtle turn of the wrist activates additional muscle fibers neglected in other triceps movements.

4. You should keep your elbows close to your body in all exercises for the triceps. This will prevent your shoulders and chest from taking over the performance of the movement. Moreover, because the main purpose of the triceps is to extend the elbow, you should keep your upper arm stable throughout each repetition. Isolation is the key to shaping the triceps. Attention to these two factors is essential for peak results.

Michelle Bellini: Ms. Italian Pro Fitness

Height: 5'6"

Weight: 130

P.O. Box 293, Presto, PA 15142-0293

Photo © J.M. Manion/J.M. Productions

People are always looking for a magic pill—one that will somehow transform their physique into a thing of beauty. Unfortunately, these products only exist in the movies. However, combined with proper training and nutrition, a variety of supplements can help maximize your potential.

Michelle Bellini is a staunch advocate of the selective use of supplementation. In the "off-season," she uses creatine monohydrate, a popular bodybuilding supplement, to fuel her workouts. "Creatine helps me when I'm going for that extra rep. I like the pump that it gives me while I'm training. I won't use it before a show, though, because it tends to make me retain water."

Michelle is also a big believer in protein powders. "When I'm on my competition diet, I eat a minimum of six meals a day. I take glutamine and whey protein for at least two of these meals. This helps to elevate my metabolism and improve my immune function."

When training for a contest, Michelle takes several supplements to help her get more defined. She specifically cites the benefits of thermogenic aids such as ephedra. "As you get closer to a show, your energy levels get depleted. I find thermogenic formulas help me to lose those last few pounds without losing muscle. They also help to keep me going when I'm dieting down. I know some people have a negative attitude about these supplements, but I think they've gotten a bad rap. The problems associated with them are usually due to misuse."

A few weeks before a show, Michelle adds several other supplements to the mix in order to maximize definition. "I take vanadyl sulfate and chromium picolinate, which help to increase insulin sensitivity and function. I feel these products help to make me a little harder. I also use l-carnitine to aid in fat-burning."

Michelle concedes that supplements are only a small part of the fitness equation. "Supplements won't be of much benefit if you don't eat and train properly. But for someone who's looking to get the most out of their physique, they can help to give you an extra edge."

Michelle's training tip

"Intensity is everything. Your body simply won't respond without an intense degree of training effort."

TARGETED WORKOUTS FOR THE TRICEPS

WORKOUT	EXERCISE	SETS
1	Nosebreakers (p. 44) supersetted with close-grip bench presses (p. 46)	2
	One-arm overhead dumbbell extensions (p. 70)	3

WORKOUT	EXERCISE	SETS
2	Triceps pressdowns (p. 45) supersetted with crossbench dips (p. 128)	2
	Overhead rope extensions (p. 72)	3

WORKOUT	EXERCISE	SETS
3	Triceps machine dips (p. 128)	2
	Two-arm overhead dumbbell extensions (p. 124)	3
	Cable kickbacks (p. 126)	3

WORKOUT	EXERCISE	SETS
4	Machine overhead extensions (p. 125)	3
	One-arm reverse pressdowns (p. 45)	3
	Dumbbell kickbacks (p. 126)	3

Triceps Exercises

TWO-ARM OVERHEAD DUMBBELL EXTENSIONS

Grasp one dumbbell with both hands. Bend your elbows and hang the weight behind your head as far as comfortably possible. Slowly straighten your arms, keeping your elbows back and pointed to the ceiling throughout the move. Contract your triceps. Slowly lower to the starting position.

Triceps Exercises

MACHINE OVERHEAD EXTENSIONS

Sit in an overhead triceps machine. Grasp the bar with your palms turned away from you. Bend your elbows and hang your hands behind your head as far as comfortably possible. Slowly straighten your arms, keeping your elbows back and pointed to the ceiling throughout the move. Contract your triceps. Return to the starting position.

Triceps Exercises

DUMBBELL KICKBACKS

Support yourself on your left knee and left hand on a flat bench. Keep your torso parallel to the floor. Grasp a dumbbell with your right hand and press your right arm against your side with your elbow at a 90-degree angle. With your palm turned toward you, straighten your arm until it is parallel with the floor. Return to the starting position. Repeat with your left arm after finishing the desired reps on your right.

Cable Kickbacks

Follow the directions for dumbbell kickbacks, except stand with your feet together and use a loop handle attachment on a low cable pulley instead of a dumbbell.

Triceps Exercises

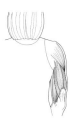

TRICEPS DIPS

Plant your heels on the floor and your hands on the edge of a flat bench, keeping your arms straight. Slowly bend your elbows as far as comfortably possible, lowering your butt below the level of the bench. Keep your elbows close to your body through the move. Straighten your arms, returning to the starting position.

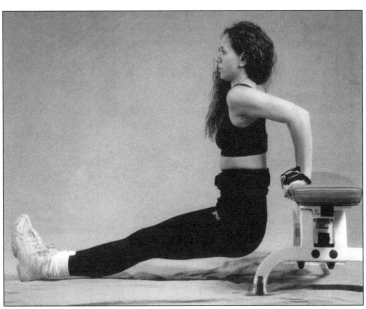

TRICEPS DIPS (continued)

Crossbench Dips

Place two flat benches roughly three feet apart. Place the heels of your feet on one flat bench and your hands on the edge of the other, keeping your arms straight. Slowly bend your elbows as far as comfortably possible, allowing your butt to descend below the level of the benches. Keep your elbows close to your body through the move. Reverse direction and straighten your arms, returning to the starting position.

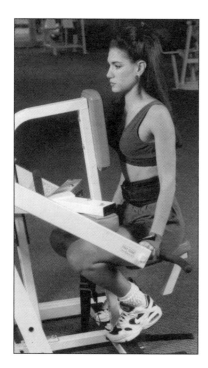

Triceps Machine Dips

Sit in a triceps dip machine and fasten the seat belt. Grasp the handles with your palms facing each other. Keeping your elbows at your sides, slowly press the handles down until your arms are straight. Contract your triceps. Reverse direction, returning to the starting position.

11 Defined Quads

Shapely thighs define the female physique. No other body part attracts more attention from the opposite sex. A great pair of legs radiates femininity and allows you to wear the shortest of skirts with confidence.

Regrettably, many women are hesitant to train their thighs with sufficient intensity. High-intensity training, they reason, will make their lower bodies thick and bulky. By following the protocols of this routine, however, your legs will not only display beautiful shape but become leaner in appearance. You will strip away excess body fat and reveal a set of tight, defined thighs.

Bodysculpting Routine

The majority of the frontal thigh is made up of the quadriceps muscles. As the name implies, the quadriceps is composed of four distinct muscles (the rectus femoris, vastus medialis, vastus lateralis, and vastus intermedius). Although the use of different angles is limited in quadriceps movements, you can use a variety of exercises to emphasize various aspects of the frontal leg. Consequently, exercises for the quadriceps are classified by their influence on each of the quadriceps muscles.

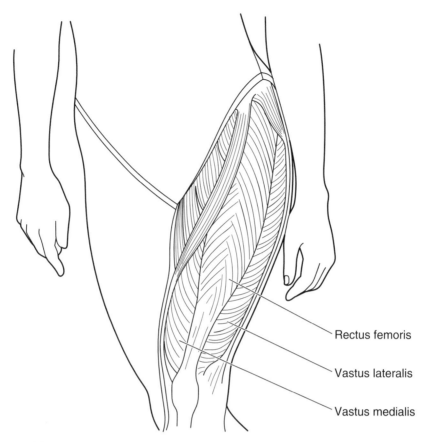

Rectus femoris

Vastus lateralis

Vastus medialis

Muscles of the leg: quadriceps.

Form

Under the High-Energy Fitness system, it is essential to use strict form during exercise performance. This will guarantee that you direct stress to the target muscles, minimizing the involvement of supporting muscles. If you lift a weight improperly, alternative muscles take stress away from the muscle you intend to work. Repeated use of poor form can result in disproportionate development. Worse, connective tissue (tendons and ligaments) often unduly assists in the movement. This is counterproductive to achieving ideal muscle tone and increases the possibility of injury.

Furthermore, "cheat" repetitions are not advised. A cheat repetition uses supporting muscles for assistance, allowing you to finish a repetition that would ordinarily be impossible. By using supporting muscles, you are cheating to complete the lift. This technique is beneficial mainly for adding mass and increasing strength. Although cheat repetitions have utility in a bodybuilding context, they will produce an outcome contrary to your fitness goals. Therefore, I do not recommend their use.

- *Class one—squats, leg presses, and lunges.* These compound movements place direct stress on the quadriceps and secondary emphasis on the hamstrings, glutes, and tie-in muscles of the legs. Each of these exercises has unique qualities that complement one another in stimulating a wide array of muscle fibers. Moreover, each movement has variations that allow you to apply additional variety to the thighs.

- *Class two—leg extensions, front kicks, adductor exercises, and body-weight movements.* These exercises include both isolation and aerobic-oriented compound movements. The isolation movements (front kicks and leg extensions) target specific parts of the quadriceps while applying only minimal stimulation to other areas. The body-weight exercises heighten your body's ability to burn fat while etching detail into the frontal thighs.

Bodysculpting Tips

1. For complete development, you should choose at least one compound and one isolation movement each workout. Then, assess your physique and round out your routine with a complementary exercise or two. If you are looking for more overall shape in your quadriceps, you may want to include another compound movement. Alternatively, to heighten your aerobic effect and increase definition, add nonweighted exercises like sissy squats and walking lunges. These can be especially effective in a giant set.

2. The lower portion of the quadriceps is most active in exercises that involve bending the knee. It is common for women to have fat deposits around the knee, reducing shape and hardness. Adding muscle tone can define this area and accentuate your proportions. Exercises such as leg extensions will isolate the quadriceps, especially the vastus muscles.

3. The upper portion of the quadriceps (rectus femoris) is more active in movements that involve bending the hip. The front kick is one of the few movements to exclude the knee joint in exercise performance, thereby stressing the upper quadriceps in relative isolation. The upper thigh is one of the more difficult areas to develop. You must apply significant effort to improve this area.

4. During squats and leg presses, you can alter the stress to the inner and outer thighs by varying the placement of your feet. Angling your toes outward can shift the emphasis of the movement to the inner portion of your thigh by increasing the stretch to the vastus medialis. Alternatively, pointing your toes inward can enhance the shape of your outer thigh due to an increased stretch of the vastus lateralis. The benefits of changing foot positions are subtle, though, and the overall effect will be limited. Do not exaggerate these foot positions, because doing so can damage the knee.

5. Make sure you do not lock out your knees on any quadriceps movement. Locking the knees reduces stimulation to the target muscles and, more importantly, places undue stress on the knee joint. The ligaments in this area are weak (especially the anterior cruciate ligament) and easily torn by the shearing forces you apply when locking the knee.

6. The inner thighs are problematic for many women. While the adductor (inner thigh) machine is the most popular exercise for toning this area, movements such as adductor cable pulls and side lunges are equally effective. As with all exercises, maintaining variety is paramount to achieving results. Accordingly, make sure to alternate among these and other movements.

TARGETED WORKOUTS FOR THE QUADRICEPS

WORKOUT 1	EXERCISE	SETS
	Leg presses (p. 47) supersetted with walking lunges (p. 134)	3
	Machine squats (p. 138)	2
	Machine adductions (p. 135)	3

WORKOUT 2	EXERCISE	SETS
	Squats (p. 48) supersetted with leg extensions (p. 137) and sissy squats (p. 74)	3

WORKOUT 3	EXERCISE	SETS
	Front squats (p. 48)	2
	Lunges (p. 133)	2
	Adductor cable pulls (p. 136)	3
	One-leg extensions (p. 137)	3

WORKOUT 4	EXERCISE	SETS
	Hack squats (p. 49) supersetted with jump squats (p. 138)	3
	Side lunges (p. 134)	3
	Front kicks (p. 73)	2

Quadriceps Exercises

LUNGES

Grasp two dumbbells. With your feet shoulder-width apart, place your right foot back and your left foot forward a comfortable distance. Keeping your right heel elevated, slowly drop your right knee, stopping just before it touches the floor. Hold your body erect through the move and don't push your left knee past the level of your toe. After finishing the desired reps, move your right foot forward and your left foot back and repeat.

Quadriceps Exercises

LUNGES *(continued)*

Walking Lunges

Stand in an open area with your feet shoulder-width apart. Take a long stride forward with your right leg, bringing your left knee to just above floor level. Keep your shoulders back and your head up through the move. Step forward with your left leg, bringing your right knee toward the ground. Alternate legs for the desired repetitions.

Side Lunges

Stand with your feet slightly wider than shoulder-width apart. Grasp two dumbbells. Hold one in front of you and the other behind you. Keeping your left leg straight, slowly bend your left knee to the side until your left thigh is parallel to the floor. Slowly rise and repeat the process immediately with your right leg.

Quadriceps Exercises

MACHINE ADDUCTIONS

Sit in an adductor machine and, with your legs apart, place your inner thighs on the restraint pads. Slowly force your legs together, contracting your inner thighs as the pads touch. Return to the starting position.

Quadriceps Exercises

ADDUCTOR CABLE PULLS

Attach a cuff to a low cable pulley and to your left ankle. With your left side to the weight stack, grasp the machine for support. Slowly pull your left leg toward and across the midline of your body, as far to your right as possible. Contract your inner thigh. Return to the starting position. Repeat with your right leg after finishing the desired reps on your left.

Quadriceps Exercises

LEG EXTENSIONS

Sit in a leg extension machine. Bend your knees and place your feet under the roller pad at the bottom of the machine. Grasp the handles. Slowly lift your feet until your legs are almost parallel to the ground. Contract your quads. Return to the starting position.

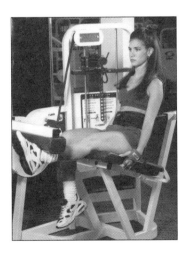

One-Leg Extensions

Follow the directions for leg extensions, except work your left leg first. Repeat with your right leg after finishing the desired reps on your left.

Quadriceps Exercises

SQUATS

See instructions and photos of squats on page 48.

Machine Squats

Follow the directions for squats (page 48), except rest a straight bar on a Smith machine high on the back of your neck. Grasp the bar with both hands and place your feet shoulder-width apart slightly in front of you. Slowly lower your body until your thighs are parallel to the ground. Slightly arch your lower back and keep your heels on the floor. When you reach a "seated" position, straighten your legs and return to the starting position.

Jump Squats

Stand with your feet shoulder-width apart. Keeping your torso erect, slowly bend your knees, sinking into a "seated" position. When your thighs are parallel with the ground, jump into the air as high as possible. Land upright, slightly bending your knees to absorb the shock.

12 Lean Hamstrings and Glutes

Without question, women have more trouble toning their butts and hamstrings than any other muscle group. This is the first place women tend to store body fat, making it especially difficult to keep firm. Worse, this area is prone to cellulite, giving the dreaded "cottage cheese" appearance to your backside.

Training will not by itself reduce excess adipose in your hamstrings and butt. As I noted earlier (see page 22), you cannot spot-reduce body fat. By combining training with a proper nutritional regimen, however, you can sculpt these muscles to create an enviable posterior. If your butt is flat, you can add shape to give it a rounded appearance. If your hamstrings are loose, you can tone them to achieve a rock-hard look. Regardless of your present condition, with a little hard work and effort, a firm, shapely backside can be yours.

Bodysculpting Routine

You can activate the hamstrings at both the hip and knee joints, but the glutes only at the hip. Thus, the hamstrings and glutes will be classified into movements that train both muscle complexes and exercises that target each complex individually.

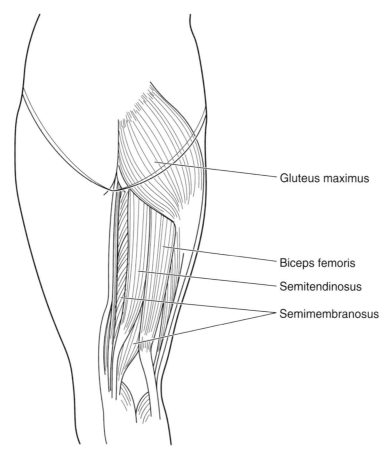

Muscles of the upper leg and buttocks.

• *Class one—stiff-legged deadlifts, good mornings, and hyperextensions.* Although they use only one joint (the hip) in performance, these exercises are compound movements in disguise. The lower back (spinal erectors), glutes, and hamstrings are all involved in the execution of these exercises. To maximize the stress to the hamstring and glutes, you must focus on contracting this area on each repetition (although the lower back will still be involved to some extent).

• *Class two—leg curls.* These isolation movements focus on the hamstrings, with minimal stress on the glutes and lower back (the calves also play a small, secondary role in exercise performance). Leg curls provide several alternatives (standing, seated, kneeling, sitting), and you can perform them using both legs or one at a time.

• *Class three—glute kicks and abductor exercises.* These isolation exercises primarily stress the glutes, with minimal emphasis on the hamstrings. You can use weighted or nonweighted movements, depending on your desire to add shape to this area.

Bodysculpting Tips

1. You should be careful using any of the exercises in class one if you have previously injured your lower back. The muscles of the lower back (spinal erectors) are highly involved in the performance of these movements and can receive undue stress, especially when you use weights. If this is a concern, you should employ nonweighted versions of these movements (particularly hyper-

extensions) that will safely stimulate the hamstrings and glutes while simultaneously strengthening the muscles of the lower back.

2.   To exact proper stress on your glutes, you must concentrate on contracting these muscles on every repetition. Women generally have difficulty understanding how to contract their glutes properly during exercise performance. The way you perform this exercise will profoundly affect the amount of stress you apply to this area. If you have doubts about this concept, practice the movement without weights until it becomes second nature.

3.   An excellent way to increase muscle tone to the glutes is to supplement your training with butt squeezes (this method is called isotension). This technique is both effective and extremely convenient. You can perform them almost anywhere, including when you are on the couch watching television, in line at the supermarket, or in bed before sleep. Simply contract your glute muscles, hold the squeeze for as long as possible (aim for 30 seconds or more), then release. After you are comfortable with this technique, try to incorporate them into sets, counting each squeeze as one repetition. Perform three sets of 15 repetitions several times a week and you will soon have buns of steel!

Janis Saffell: National Aerobics Champion, Star of ESPN2's "Crunch Fitness"

Height: 5'7"

Weight: 125

14932 Paddock Drive, Wellington, FL 33414

Janis Saffell lives by the phrase: "Variety is the spice of life." As one of America's leading aerobics instructors, she continually applies this dictum to her cardio routine. "I'm always striving to keep my body off-guard, challenging myself to reach new heights. I never want my body to get used to an aerobic activity."

While Janis employs a variety of different activities in her workout, her favorite form of aerobics is cardio-kickboxing. "I warm up by jumping rope for a short period of time. After finishing the warm-up, I gradually pick up the intensity. First, I start with some punching patterns; then, I go into different kick patterns; and finally, I mix up the arms and legs into various combinations. It's the best cardio workout that I've ever done."

Janis especially likes the fact that kickboxing is dynamic. "Kickboxing utilizes a tremendous variety of moves. You're not doing the same thing over and over again, like most of the other cardio modalities. It also incorporates so many different muscle groups. Your arms, shoulders, abs, legs all are involved in the workout. This helps you see results in a matter of weeks."

Janis also points to the ancillary benefits associated with kickboxing. "Kickboxing provides much more than just fat burning. It gives you agility, stability, and coordination—things that are really important in everyday functionality. And the best thing about it is that there is virtually no choreography involved, so you don't have to be self-conscious that you're too clumsy to perform the moves. Literally everyone can enjoy its benefits."

Consistent with her cross-training philosophy, Janis advises that you regularly change your routine. "The best thing to do is to combine kickboxing with traditional forms of cardio. In this way, you'll never get into a training rut."

Photo courtesy of Janis Saffell, International Fitness Expert

Janis' training tip

"Fitness has to be fun. If you don't enjoy it, you're not going to do it!"

TARGETED WORKOUTS FOR THE HAMSTRINGS AND GLUTES

WORKOUT	EXERCISE	SETS
1	Stiff-legged deadlifts (p. 51)	2
	Standing cable leg curls (p. 75)	2
	Machine abductions (p. 144)	3

WORKOUT	EXERCISE	SETS
2	Hyperextensions (p. 146) supersetted with lying leg curls (p. 52)	3
	Butt blasters (p. 145)	3

WORKOUT	EXERCISE	SETS
3	Reverse hyperextensions (p. 146)	3
	Kneeling leg curls (p. 147)	3
	Cable back kicks (p. 148)	2

WORKOUT	EXERCISE	SETS
4	Good mornings (p. 50)	3
	Seated leg curls (p. 52) supersetted with machine abductions (p. 144)	2

Hamstring-Glute Exercises

MACHINE ABDUCTIONS

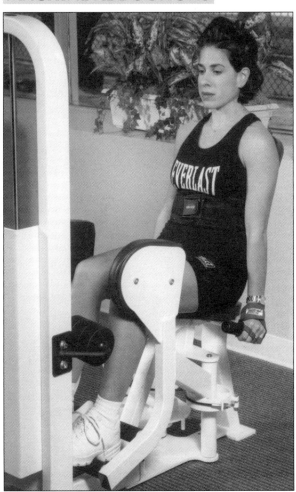

Sit at an abductor machine and, with your legs together, place your outer thighs on the restraint pads. Slowly force your legs apart as far as comfortably possible. Contract your glutes. Return to the starting position.

Hamstring-Glute Exercises

BUTT BLASTERS

Kneel in a butt blaster machine. Place your forearms on the arm pads and your left foot on the footplate. Slowly push back your left leg; stop just short of locking your knee. Contract your glutes. Return to the starting position. Repeat with your right leg after finishing the desired reps on your left.

Hamstring-Glute Exercises

HYPEREXTENSIONS

Lie on your stomach in a Roman chair with your thighs on the restraint pad and your heels under the rollers. Fold your hands across your chest and arch your lower back. Slowly rise until you are almost parallel to the floor. Contract your glutes. Return to the starting position.

Reverse Hyperextensions

Follow the directions for hyperextensions, except lie face down on a flat bench with your lower torso hanging off the end, feet almost touching the floor. Grasp the bench with both hands. Slowly raise your feet until they are almost parallel to the ground.

Hamstring-Glute Exercises

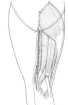

KNEELING LEG CURLS

Kneel in a kneeling leg curl machine, your left heel under the roller pad. Place your forearms on the restraint pads for support. Slowly curl your left foot; stop just short of touching your butt or as far as comfortably possible. Contract your left hamstring. Return to the starting position. Repeat with your right leg after finishing the desired reps on your left.

Hamstring-Glute Exercises

CABLE BACK KICKS

Attach a cuff to a low cable pulley and to your right ankle. Face the weight stack and grasp a sturdy part of the machine for support. Slowly bring your right leg back as far as comfortably possible without moving your upper torso. Contract your glutes. Slowly return to the starting position. Repeat with your left leg after finishing the desired reps on your right.

13 Diamond Calves

In everyday life you use your calves more than any other muscle complex. You activate them every time you walk, run, climb stairs, or perform any other ambulatory movement. Whenever you are on your feet, your calves endure muscular stimulus.

Although frequently overlooked in the scheme of a training routine, diamond-shaped calves significantly augment your body lines. They contour your lower legs and complement the overall shape of your physique. In addition, they help give the illusion of leaner looking thighs—a welcome side benefit for most women. Once you have defined these muscles, you'll see why diamonds really are a girl's best friend.

Bodysculpting Routine

Although the complete area of the calves consists of ten small muscles, just two—the soleus and gastrocnemius—are the show muscles that most readily create optimal calf shape. Two basic positions shift the emphasis to these muscles—one with legs straight and the other with knees bent. Hence, exercises for the calves are classified by the amount of stress you apply to each muscle.

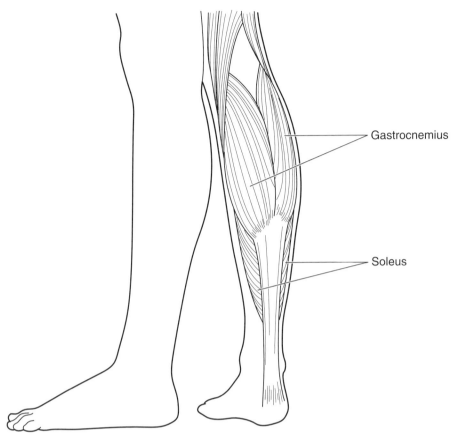

Muscles of the calf.

• *Class one—standing raises, donkey raises, and toe presses.* These exercises use a straight-legged stance and thus place more stress on the gastrocnemius muscle. This is the largest of the calf muscles and the most important for bodysculpting.

• *Class two—seated raises.* These exercises require you to bend at the knees, thereby heightening emphasis on the soleus muscle. The soleus, for the most part, is hidden behind the gastrocnemius. When properly developed, however, it adds fullness and contour to the calves. Virtually all the muscle fibers of the soleus are endurance-oriented (roughly 80 percent), making it extremely difficult to shape.

Bodysculpting Tips

1.   Contrary to popular belief, there is little benefit to turning your calves in or out during exercise performance. But by rolling onto the sides of your feet, however, you can shift the emphasis to different parts of the calf. Rolling your feet toward the big toe tends to stress the inner portion of the calf. This gives your calves a diamond-shaped appearance and creates in this area the illusion of increased dimension. Alternatively, rolling toward your little toe emphasizes the outer head, accentuating the definition of your calves.

2.   Be careful to remain under control on the negative portion of any calf exercise. As your heel lowers to the floor, you will stretch your Achilles tendon, applying a great deal of force to this area. You can severely injure your Achilles tendon if you are not careful. Always lower slowly on the negative movement without bouncing and stretch only to the point that the muscle allows.

3. Because you use them in everyday activities, the calves are endurance-oriented muscles that respond stubbornly to training. Depending on genetics, the calves are often the most difficult muscles to shape and define. Accordingly, they can often benefit from higher repetitions than normal (as many as 30 per set). Because of the high percentage of endurance fibers in the calves, high repetitions can penetrate the muscle more effectively than in other muscle groups, thereby improving results.

4. Make sure to stretch the calves between each set. Only one major artery feeds each of the calf muscles (the sural artery feeds the gastrocnemius and the posterior tibial artery feeds the soleus). Thus, blood flow tends to be reduced to this area during training. This causes metabolic waste such as lactic acid to accrue rapidly and increases the potential for muscular cramping. Stretching will help flush waste from the calves and decrease cramping.

5. As with the biceps, you cannot alter the length of your calf muscles through training. If your calf muscle is short and sits high on your lower leg, there is little you can do to increase its length (sorry again, but that's the way it is!). But by developing the soleus muscle (which extends into the lower region of the calves) you can add depth in this area, creating the impression of a longer muscle.

6. As a supplement to training, wearing high heels can add additional shape and definition to the calf muscles. They place the calves in a flexed position for extended periods, thereby forcing the calf muscles to endure protracted stress. Because of the endurance nature of the calves, they will be forced to adapt to this stress to prevent muscular fatigue. The effect will be an increase in the definition of your calves.

TARGETED WORKOUTS FOR THE CALVES

WORKOUT	EXERCISE	SETS
1	Machine toe presses (p. 154)	3
	Seated calf raises (p. 153)	3

WORKOUT	EXERCISE	SETS
2	Donkey calf raises (p. 155)	3
	One-legged seated calf raises (p. 153)	3

WORKOUT	EXERCISE	SETS
3	Donkey calf raises (p. 155) supersetted with toe presses (p. 53)	3
	One-legged seated calf raises (p. 153)	2

WORKOUT	EXERCISE	SETS
4	Machine toe presses (p. 154)	3
	Seated calf raises (p. 153)	3

Calf Exercises

SEATED CALF RAISES

Sit in a seated calf machine and place the restraint pads tightly across your thighs. Place the balls of your feet on the footplate and drop your heels as far below your toes as possible. Slowly rise as high as you can onto your toes until your calves are fully flexed. Contract your calves. Return to the starting position.

One-Legged Seated Calf Raises

Follow the directions for seated calf raises, except work your left leg first. Repeat with your right leg after finishing the desired reps on your left.

Calf Exercises

MACHINE TOE PRESSES

Sit in a toe press machine, pressing your back firmly into the padded seat. Place your toes at the bottom of the footplate a comfortable distance apart. Straighten your legs and drop your heels as far behind your toes as possible. Keeping your knees stable, slowly press your toes up as far as you can. Contract your calves. Slowly reverse direction, returning to the starting position.

Calf Exercises

DONKEY CALF RAISES

Place your middle back on the restraint pad of a donkey calf machine. Place the balls of your feet on the footplate and drop your heels below your toes. Slowly rise as high as you can onto your toes until your calves are fully flexed. Contract your calves. Return to the starting position.

Karen Hulse: Women's World Pro Fitness Champion

Height: 5'4"

Weight: 119

P.O. Box 293, Presto, PA 15142-0293

Photo © J.M. Manion/J.M. Productions

Anyone who complains that their schedule doesn't allow them to get in a workout should talk to Karen Hulse. Not only is Karen one of the leading fitness competitors in the world, but she also works a full-time job as a sales representative. How does she find time to maintain a great physique? "I meticulously plan my week out in advance and structure my workout and meals accordingly," states Karen.

Her training program is split into two parts, working around her day job. "I always get up early in the morning and do my aerobics—anywhere from 45 minutes to an hour—and then go to work from nine to five. I usually get back to the gym around six o'clock and train whatever body parts are on my schedule for that day. If I have an upcoming competition, I'll also practice my fitness routine about three times a week."

Karen is equally disciplined with her nutritional regimen. "On Sunday night, I'll prepare all of my meals for the upcoming week. Once they're cooked, I'll package them in Tupperware and place them in the refrigerator so they're ready to go. This way, I don't have to worry about straying from my diet and can maintain my physique year round."

As someone who is constantly on the road, Karen also has to deal with the challenges of being limited in what she can do. "When I'm traveling, I often won't have a place where I can work out. If this is the case, I'll bring along a set of elastic strength bands and restructure my routine according to my schedule. By combining the strength bands with body-weight exercises like push-ups and dips, I can actually get a pretty good workout and not lose anything while I'm away."

While other women find reasons to justify their lack of physical activity, Karen takes a proactive stance. "I never let work be an excuse for not getting in my workouts. If you're determined to stay fit, you find a way to make it work."

Karen's training tip

"Everything should be done in moderation. Take one day out of the week and make it a 'cheat' day. As long as you don't go overboard, you'll still be able to maintain a great physique."

14 Six-Pack Abs

The abdominals are the showcase of your physique. Because they lie in the center of your body, they are the first place that draws attention when you wear a bikini. Midriff shirts, crop-tops, and other garments are designed to flaunt this sensual area. For many women, however, a flat, toned stomach is elusive due to genetic factors.

Women tend to find the lower abdominal region the most problematic. As I am sure you are aware, your menstrual cycle results in a significant amount of water retention each month. Your body adapts by stretching the muscle in this area outward. Childbearing can further distend the pelvic muscles. Because this portion of your abdominals is much thinner than the upper portion, the muscle can apply only limited resistance to this response. Therefore, the lower abdominals become softer and more pliable, ultimately causing a slight bulge in the pelvic region.

Despite these considerations, targeted bodysculpting can help you develop a great set of abs. Once you strip away abdominal body fat, it is rather easy to bring out detail in this region. With a dedicated routine, your midsection will readily take shape, achieving a lean, washboard appearance.

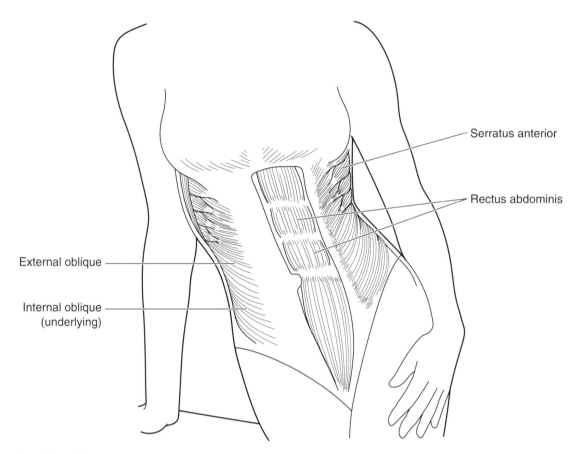

Serratus anterior

Rectus abdominis

External oblique

Internal oblique
(underlying)

Muscles of the abdomen.

Bodysculpting Routine

The abdominals are one long sheath of muscle that runs from just underneath your chest (sternum) all the way down into your pelvis. Thus, you cannot separate the upper and lower abdominals or train one part without affecting the entire muscle. You can, however, apply more stress to the upper or lower abdominals by lifting from either the chest or the pelvis, respectively. Consequently, abdominal exercises will be classified by their emphasis on the upper and lower abdominal regions.

• *Class one—crunches.* These movements put maximal stress on the upper portion of the abdominals. When executing crunches, you must concentrate on pulling your chest downward toward your hips. Your lower back should never come off the floor. If it does, you will activate your hip flexor muscles at the expense of your abdominals.

• *Class two—leg raises and reverse crunches.* These movements focus more on the lower portion of the abdominals. As noted, the lower abdominals are one of the most troublesome muscles for a woman to develop. Because of the proximity of the muscles in this region, they are difficult to isolate. Compounding this problem, the lower abdominals have limited range of motion, making contraction a chore. This severely hampers your ability to tone this area. To work the lower abs most effectively, you should concentrate on raising the pelvis up toward your stomach—not simply raising and lowering your legs.

Variation

I am often asked, "What is the *best* exercise for the abs?" or "What is the *best* exercise for the buttocks?" The answer is that there is no one best exercise. I already have noted that changing the angle of an exercise will stimulate different fibers in a muscle. You can also improve your results simply by using a variation of the same exercise. The barbell press, for example, is a fine exercise for developing the muscles of the chest. By alternating to a flat dumbbell press in your next workout, you can exert a different stimulus on the same muscle. Switch to a machine press for an even different feel.

Variation counteracts the adaptation process that takes place when you regularly apply the same stress to your body. The human body is adaptive. When you continually use the same exercises, your body begins to develop a tolerance. Ultimately, you will reach a plateau in your training. By constantly varying the exercises in your routine, your muscles will never be able to adapt to a particular exercise and will thus continue to improve.

Furthermore, some exercises are better suited to certain body types. For instance, taller people tend to have more difficulty performing squats because of the long range of motion required. Therefore, consider your body characteristics when choosing exercises. Numerous exercises are available for each muscle group, and many of them are more or less interchangeable. Although this book provides sample routines with suggested exercise combinations, the specific exercises you use are up to you. Once you familiarize yourself with High-Energy Fitness and gain some training experience, you should be able to substitute various exercises at will. As long as you understand the purpose of an exercise, you can create a varied routine that will allow you to progress continuously. In the end, you should choose an assortment of exercises that best accentuates your body structure, and then mold these exercises into a cohesive format.

Bodysculpting Tips

1. Although training the abdominals will not give you a flat stomach, you can promote additional fat burning by performing your entire abdominal routine as one giant set, taking virtually no rest between exercises. Because the abdominals are a flat sheath of muscle tissue, your ability to shape them is limited. Thus, your objective should be to achieve hardness and definition in this area, while shedding body fat to make them visible. This, in turn, creates less need for resting between sets. If possible, choose three exercises and attempt to move directly from one to the next—in essence, performing nine sets successively. If you must rest between sets, do so only enough to catch your breath (no more than five seconds).

2. When performing crunches, you should make sure to tuck your chin to your chest and put your hands across your body—not behind your head. You may tend to pull from the neck when your hands are behind your head, especially when you begin to approach failure. This not only reduces stress to the abdominals but also can cause a strain to the muscles in the neck.

3. I generally recommend that you avoid performing weighted movements for the sides of the abdominals (obliques). Exercises like weighted side bends will contribute to a blocky appearance in your waist. This is one area of the body where adding even a little bit of muscle can be detrimental to your overall proportions. If you wish to train this area, nonweighted exercises, such as side twists, work best for toning (although they have limited utility).

4. Abdominal machines (such as the Gutbuster) do not provide any additional benefit over traditional exercises. They can, however, make the performance of these movements somewhat easier, which can be helpful if you have weak abdominal muscles. They are not a panacea, though, and will not make your stomach any flatter, as often advertised.

TARGETED WORKOUTS FOR THE ABDOMINALS

WORKOUT	EXERCISE	SETS
1	Crunches (p. 54) supersetted with side twists (p. 161) and hanging leg raises (p. 162)	3
2	Rope crunches (p. 76) supersetted with incline crunches (p. 163) and bench leg raises (p. 55)	3
3	Machine crunches (p. 163) supersetted with twisting crunches (p. 54) and reverse crunches (p. 77)	3
4	Seated rope crunches (p. 76) supersetted with knee-ins (p. 56) and twisting hanging leg raises (p. 162)	3

Abdominal Exercises

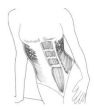

SIDE TWISTS

Rest a bodybar behind your neck across your shoulders. Grasp each end of the bar. Slowly twist your upper body to the right, contracting your oblique muscles as you turn. Reverse direction and twist your body all the way to the left. Only your waist should move; keep your hips stationary. In order to reduce torque to your neck, look straight ahead and do not turn your head.

Abdominal Exercises

HANGING LEG RAISES

With your hands shoulder-width apart, grasp a chinning bar. Keep your upper torso motionless through the move. Slightly bend your knees and slowly raise your legs so that your pelvis tilts toward your stomach. Contract your abs. Return to the starting position.

Twisting Hanging Leg Raises

Follow the directions for hanging leg raises, except twist your legs to the right when you raise them. Repeat to the left after performing the desired reps to the right.

Abdominal Exercises

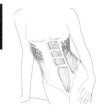

CRUNCHES

See instructions and photos of crunches on page 54.

Incline Crunches

Follow the directions for crunches on page 54, except lie on an incline bench with your feet secured and your head at the bottom of the incline. Your thighs should be perpendicular to the ground, your hands folded across your chest. Slowly raise your chest toward your knees, shortening your trunk.

Machine Crunches

Follow the directions for crunches on page 54, except lie in a crunch machine with your feet hooked under the restraints. Keep your thighs perpendicular to the ground. Slowly raise your chest toward your knees, shortening your trunk.

Debbie Kruck: Ms. Fitness USA

Height: 5'6"

Weight: 130

P.O. Box 2026, Ormond Beach, FL 32175

A common belief is that all fitness models are born with great bodies. As in the case of Debbie Kruck, however, perception is not always consistent with reality.

As a teenager, Debbie was not at all petite. "Before I started training, I weighed 170 pounds and wore a size-14 dress," says Debbie. "I tried all the fad diets, aerobic classes, and tapes there were, but really didn't see my body change."

Despite her fitness failures, Debbie was committed to redefining her physique. "Whatever I did was always extreme. At one point, I went on one of those liquid diets and did nothing but drink powdered shakes

Photo courtesy of Debbie Kruck

for two weeks. I ended up getting really sick and had to go to the hospital. But that aspect of my personality was what drove me to succeed."

One day, while reading a popular fitness magazine, Debbie experienced a revelation that changed her life. "I was browsing through some magazines and saw an article about a woman named Chris Glass, who was a lightweight national physique champion. She had lost a great deal of weight, and I instantly related to her situation. The article included pictures of her when she was overweight and out-of-shape, and then showed her transformation into this beautiful body. That's when it hit me that I could change my overall shape rather than just continuing along the same dead-end path that I was taking.

"Thereafter, I turned to weight training and developed a sound nutritional philosophy. Within a short period of time, my body started to take shape and looked better than it ever did. I just kept plugging away and the rest is history."

Today, Debbie is 50 pounds lighter and wears a size-4 dress. And for those who think that becoming strong and shapely is only a pipe dream, Debbie has these words: "Everyone has the ability to change their body. You never know what you can accomplish until you try."

Debbie's training tip

"Less can be more. Too often, women stay in the gym for hours without really accomplishing much. Train smart and you'll get better results."

15 Fat Burning With Aerobics

Cardiovascular exercise is an essential component of any comprehensive training regimen. This is especially true when your eventual goal is to develop lean muscle tone. For the majority of women, aerobics alone make up their workouts. Many have never attempted any type of weight training, but virtually all have taken part in some form of aerobic exercise. Women seem to form a kinship with aerobics, believing it to be the key to a great body. Here, a little knowledge can be a dangerous thing. You will not achieve your desired results simply by throwing together a cardio routine. To obtain proper benefits, you must assess your needs and appropriately integrate aerobics into your fitness program. Contrary to popular belief, there is more to aerobic training than merely running on a treadmill or riding a stationary bike. In fact, science underlies the performance of cardiovascular activities, and proper implementation can have a profound impact on your overall results.

Simply stated, an aerobic exercise is any activity that requires your body to use oxygen during exercise performance (as opposed to anaerobic exercise, which does not consume oxygen). This is generally accompanied by a corresponding elevation in resting heart rate and an increase in vascular blood flow. From a bodysculpting perspective, aerobics serve a dual purpose: they improve muscular endurance and burn body fat. Essentially, aerobics complement your weight-training regimen, working synergistically to help you achieve total fitness.

Although the health benefits of cardiovascular exercise are well known, the way in which aerobics interact with the bodysculpting process is not as well understood. Besides knowing that they help burn calories, most women have a poor comprehension of the effect that aerobics have on their physiques. To get a better handle on the way that cardio affects your bodysculpting endeavors, let's explore its benefits:

• *Cardiovascular exercise expedites fat burning.* Aerobic fitness causes your mitochondria (cellular furnaces where fat burning takes place) to expand in size and number as well as increase the amount of aerobic enzymes (chemicals that accelerate the fat-burning process) within your muscle fibers. The better your aerobic conditioning, the more your muscles will become programmed to use fat rather than glycogen stores (carbohydrates) for fuel. Obviously, by increasing the efficiency with which your body burns fat as an energy source, you will be better able to reduce body-fat stores while preserving lean muscle tissue.

• *Cardiovascular exercise promotes better muscular endurance for weight training.* Your heart is the most important muscle in your body. It directly affects all your bodily functions and plays an integral role in muscular performance. Because high-energy weight training has an aerobic predilection, cardiovascular conditioning will have a direct bearing on your performance. When you lift weights, glycogen stored in your muscles turns to glucose, which, through a chemical process, converts to waste that you expel during breathing. When aerobic capacity is compromised, this chemical process is shortchanged, causing lactic acid to accumulate in your muscles. Lactic acid produces the burning sensation that inhibits muscular contractions, which can cause you to fall short of achieving your target repetition range. By increasing your cardiac capacity, you improve oxygen transport to your muscles, delaying the onset of lactic acid buildup and hence heightening your training ability.

• *Cardiovascular exercise aids in muscular recuperation.* Aerobics help to expand your network of capillaries, the tiny blood vessels that allow nutrients such as protein and carbohydrates to be absorbed into body tissues. The more capillaries you have, the more efficient your body becomes in using these nutrients for muscular repair. Capillaries also help to clear waste products, particularly carbon dioxide, from the food-burning process, further enhancing the efficiency of your nutrient delivery system. This accelerates the rate at which your muscles are able to get the resources needed for recuperation, helping to improve workouts and speed recovery.

Although the benefits of cardio are numerous, achieving them is decidedly more complicated. Women, as a whole, are at a particular disadvantage regarding aerobic training. Several distinct gender differences influence overall aerobic ability, and women consistently come up on the short end of the stick. Unlike many differences between the sexes, these discrepancies are subtle and not visually apparent. To enjoy a safe and effective workout, however, you must consider these differences when constructing your aerobic routine. The following are some of these inherent differences and their relationship to aerobic performance:

• *The aerobic capacity of a woman is roughly 10 to 20 percent lower than that of a man.* Women generally have smaller internal organs (including the heart and lungs) as well as lower hemoglobin levels than men. This results in lower cardiac output (the amount of blood pumped out of the heart in one minute), which curtails a woman's ability to deliver blood and oxygen to exercising muscles. Because aerobic exercise requires oxygen to sustain performance, endurance is compromised. Moreover, the heart and lungs help expel metabolic waste from the body, aiding in the recovery process. Because these organs are smaller in women, they do not remove waste as efficiently, thereby reducing recuperative ability. The net effect is that women have to work harder than men to achieve the same level of aerobic fitness.

• *Women have a greater potential for joint and connective tissue injury than men.* Women tend to have small bone structures that are highly susceptible to the rigors of training. Aerobic exercise can heighten the demands placed on the joints and connective tissue, making them more prone to injury. The knees are especially vulnerable because of a woman's large Q-angle (the angle formed between the knee and the outer thigh). As a rule, the wider the hips, the greater the Q-angle and, because women genetically have wider hips (to accommodate the demands of childbirth), they ordinarily will have larger Q-angles. The significance here is that larger Q-angles cause greater force to be placed on the knees during strenuous activities, substantially increasing the potential for injury to this area. Thus, women must be particularly careful in performing endurance activities that are ballistic in nature (for example, step classes and high-impact aerobics) and should stick to controlled, low-impact movements.

• *Hormonal fluctuations can compromise women's aerobic ability.* Prolonged exercise can cause dizziness, nausea, and other side effects during menstruation and menopause. Hormonal fluctuations during these times throw off the body's normal rhythms, resulting in a variety of symptoms. Obviously, this will impede cardiovascular capacity and make training more difficult. Moreover, the general discomfort that is experienced can further reduce training motivation. Some women must cope with difficult symptoms such as cramps and headaches, magnifying the importance of discipline.

Further complicating the quest for aerobic fitness is rampant misinformation. As with weight training, numerous myths relating to cardiovascular exercise somehow have been taken as gospel. By sifting through this misinformation, you will be able to develop a clear understanding of how to add cardio to your routine. To get the most out of your efforts, let us dispel some of the more common myths and explore the realities of aerobics:

MYTH: Using the stairmaster will give you a big butt.

This myth gained credence when a popular magazine suggested that the stairmaster was responsible for increasing the derrieres of exercising women across the country. Afraid that they would soon possess a rear end the size of a movie screen, women began to avoid the stairmaster. Fortunately, there is not a shred of truth to this myth. It is virtually impossible to increase muscle mass substantially through the performance of *any* endurance-related cardiovascular activity. The reason for this is simple: there are two basic types of muscle fibers, slow twitch (type I) and fast twitch (type II), and each responds to different stimuli.

© Cheyenne Rouse

Working out on a stairmaster will not increase the size of your butt.

Fast-twitch fibers are strength-related fibers that contract rapidly but are quick to fatigue. They derive most of their energy from burning glucose, rather than fat, as a fuel source. These factors make them more sensitive to weight-bearing exercises (push-ups, squats, and so on) that you use in short, intense periods of training. To accommodate the demands of anaerobic exercise, fast-twitch fibers respond by growing larger and stronger. Therefore, they are the only types of fibers that can significantly increase in size and promote muscular bulk.

Slow-twitch fibers, on the other hand, are endurance-oriented fibers that have limited ability to grow larger. These fibers get much of their energy by burning fat for fuel, contracting slowly but being able to endure extended periods of activity. Slow-twitch fibers are predominantly used during the performance of aerobic exercise, with almost no activation of fast-twitch fibers. As such, little, if any, muscular growth can take place. Because exercising on the stairmaster is aerobic, it stands to reason that it cannot contribute to building substantial muscle tissue in any part of the body, including your butt!

MYTH: You cannot overtrain by performing cardiovascular exercise.

Because cardiovascular exercise is an endurance activity executed at decreased intensity, many women feel that there is no limit to how much they can perform. However, although your body can tolerate a greater volume of aerobic exercise than anaerobic activity, too much of it will eventually set back your fitness endeavors and have a negative impact on your physique.

Although recovery ability varies among individuals, the body needs rest and recuperation to regenerate its glycogen stores. Glycogen reserves are your body's primary energy source, giving you the strength and endurance to perform everyday chores. Because cardio burns glycogen (as well as fat) during exercise performance, too much cardio will deplete these reserves, ultimately causing you to become overtrained.

Overtraining will make your body less efficient in using fat for fuel, and is apt to feed on your muscle tissue (due to a secretion of stress hormones) for energy. Moreover, it can throw off your biochemical balance, resulting in a variety of complications including cessation of your period (amenorrhea), constant fatigue, and other anomalies. Therefore, you must pay keen attention to symptoms related to overtraining, modifying your aerobic capacity according to your physical state.

MYTH: Low-intensity aerobic activities are better for fat burning than high-intensity exercise.

This myth was given credence when several research studies indicated that low-intensity activities burned a greater percentage of fat calories than high-intensity

Weight Training for Weight Loss

Weight training helps to promote fat loss. Adding muscle is the only way to increase resting metabolic rate, which directly increases the burning of fat as fuel. Thus, improving your musculature will have an immediate impact in weight reduction. Although you do not need large muscles to produce this effect, developing muscular shape and definition will increase your metabolism.

In addition, people tend to restrict their caloric intake while trying to lose weight. This can often cause the body to enter a starvation mode and begin to catabolize muscle tissue for fuel. If you neglect weight training, your metabolism will begin to slow down from the loss of muscle. This will produce a rebound effect after you no longer restrict your calorie intake; you can gain back more weight than you lost by dieting.

activities. These studies confirmed that the body prefers to use fat as its fuel source during low-intensity exercise (equating to roughly 60 percent of the calories burned, as opposed to about 40 percent from high-intensity exercise).

It is misguided, however, to believe that the selective use of fat for fuel will translate into burning more total fat calories. High-intensity exercise burns more fat calories on an absolute basis than lower-intensity activities. Because the most important aspect of training intensity is the total amount of fat calories burned—not the percentage from fat—higher-intensity exercise has the decided edge.

Furthermore, when you consider the time-related efficiency of training, low-intensity exercise provides a poor cost-benefit dividend. After all, why would you want to spend an hour running on the treadmill when you can get better results from training for half that time? In final analysis, if fat burning is your aim, performing cardiovascular exercise at high intensity is your best choice.

MYTH: Sweat is a good indicator of exercise intensity.

Most women mistakenly believe that you "gotta sweat" to have a successful workout. Although sweat is usually associated with rigorous exercise, it is not essential to achieving results.

When you exercise, sweat is brought on by an elevation of body temperature from metabolic heat. Your body regulates its temperature by activating your sweat glands, which then release water through your pores as a cooling mechanism. Thus, sweat is an indicator that your body temperature is rising, not necessarily that you are exercising at an intense level. Thus, rather than judging your workout by how much you sweat, use maximal heart rate or maximal oxygen consumption as a yardstick of how hard you are working.

Moreover, contrary to popular belief, being out of shape does not increase your propensity to sweat. In fact, the more physically fit you are, the more you will tend to perspire. Frequent exercise tends to make your sweat glands increasingly sensitive to rises in body temperature. Over time, your body begins to perceive when you are starting to exercise, and, not wanting to store extra heat, signals the sweat glands sooner than it did before you began your training program.

MYTH: Aerobic classes are the best form of cardiovascular exercise.

Mention aerobics and most women envision an instructor leading a class through various jumps, twists, and other athletic movements. These classes look fun and can be a great place to socialize and meet new people. Every week there seems to be a new gimmick, with a catchy name and a clever marketing angle—high impact, step, slide, spin—the list goes on.

Laurie Donnelly: Ms. Fitness America, Star of ESPN's "Bodyshaping"

Height: 5'3"

Weight: 118

P.O. Box 1163, Newport Beach, CA 92659

Photo courtesy of Laurie Donnelly

For any woman obsessed with her weight, Laurie Donnelly is a true role model. As a teenager, Laurie had a distorted body image, which ultimately led to a severe eating disorder. "I really had no concept of proper nutrition and was consumed with staying thin. I thought the best way to lose weight was by restricting calories and performing a lot of aerobics. My solution was to keep eating less while increasing the amount of exercise I performed."

By the age of 18, anorexia combined with gross overtraining caught up with Laurie. Her weight dwindled to 88 pounds, and she was constantly fatigued. "I was completely run down. I was doing so many high-impact aerobic classes that I ended up with multiple fractures in my shins. My body just couldn't handle all the stress being put on it. One day, I just passed out from exhaustion and my parents sent me to a doctor who discovered that my thyroid had completely shut down."

The physician prescribed Synthroid to regulate her thyroid, but this only exacerbated her situation. "I was dealing with the psychological problems of anorexia, and the Synthroid greatly elevated my metabolism. This made me hungry all the time and caused me to eat—even though I didn't want to. So I just sort of slid into bulimia."

Laurie's battle with food continued over the next few years. She went from complete deprivation to decadent overindulgence, fluctuating by as much as 40 pounds. Then, Laurie met a friend who counseled her on the virtues of eating consistently. "I was barely eating anything and doing a ton of exercise. I couldn't understand why I was skinny on top and couldn't lose weight in my legs. I knew there must be a better way, but I just couldn't figure out what to do."

The friend encouraged her to regiment her diet and eat small, frequent meals. "He told me to try—just try—eating six, balanced meals a day. My first reaction was 'There's no way that I'm going to eat that much food.' But then I started to realize that I was doing the same thing for years and not seeing any results. So I decided to give it a shot for a month and see what happened." Laurie noticed an immediate change in her physique. Within six weeks, her body fat had dropped by more than 7 percent! Laurie never turned back. "I can't overemphasize the importance of proper nutrition. Don't think you can just exercise and eat whatever you want—it just won't happen."

Laurie's training tip

"There is no magic pill for developing a terrific physique. It takes commitment and consistency—any less and you'll never reach your potential."

Unfortunately, any group fitness activity is generally inferior to a program that is specifically designed for an individual. Aerobic classes must cater to the masses and, most likely, will not optimally target your heart rate. On the other hand, individual aerobic modalities allow you to train within your target zone. Therefore, you can customize a routine to meet your specific needs, resulting in optimal fat-burning potential.

Moreover, because of the extreme, unorthodox nature of many aerobic movements performed in a class setting, the risk of injury is heightened. An injury can seriously curtail your workout regimen, potentially hampering your ability to train indefinitely. Conversely, you can execute individual modalities in a controlled fashion. Thus, they tend to be safer to perform with less potential for injury.

Aerobics classes are not without merit. Because many women are not internally motivated to exercise, these classes can provide an impetus to become more active. This, in turn, can help promote adherence to an exercise program. Hence, if you simply cannot motivate yourself to exercise, or perhaps just want to have some fun, an aerobics class might be right for you.

However, although anything that helps to increase your motivation to exercise is worthwhile, experience has shown that the best way to encourage lasting adherence is to achieve results in the safest, most expedient way possible. There is no greater motivating factor than seeing your body change before your eyes. Thus, from a cost-benefit perspective, a custom-tailored, individually designed cardiovascular regimen is the most effective way to train.

The last things to note when creating your cardiovascular routine are the philosophical differences between the aerobic and weight-training components within the High-Energy Fitness system. Although weight training in a high-energy format creates an aerobic environment, it is still, largely, an anaerobic endeavor. Weight training requires short bouts of intense training with all-out effort, culminating when you induce muscular failure. This breaks down muscle and connective tissue and overloads your central nervous system. Because of the tremendous stress to your body, you must maintain a set schedule that will provide the rest you need to regenerate bodily function.

Cardiovascular exercise, on the other hand, is basically an endurance activity (that is, an activity performed in continuous fashion for relatively long periods of time). Compared to weight training, the intensity used in these activities is moderate. The goal in aerobics is not to train to failure but to sustain a protracted elevation of heart rate and an increase in oxygen uptake. Only minimal breakdown of muscle tissue is associated with aerobic training, permitting rapid recuperation from a training session. Therefore, you can perform cardio more frequently than weight training, with less rest between sessions.

The information just covered should serve as background to the cardiovascular protocols of High-Energy Fitness. With this knowledge, you can apply these protocols in an intelligent fashion, ensuring maximum results. Bodysculpting is a scientific process that requires a well-mapped strategy to achieve your ideal physique. You, like all women, have a unique structure, and you must strive to become in tune with it. Use the following protocols as the foundation of your aerobic routine, paying special heed to the limiting factors of your abilities and body type:

- *Frequency:* How often you engage in aerobic exercise depends on your genetics and overall activity level. Most women should perform cardio three to five days a week, but personal circumstances make these guidelines somewhat variable. Assess factors such as your overall muscular conditioning and your need to lose additional body fat, adjusting the frequency of your aerobic training accordingly. As stated earlier, high-energy weight training taxes your body's resources, including your muscles, connective tissue, and central nervous system. Aerobic exercise can compound this predicament. To avoid overtraining, I recommend that you give your body at least two days a week of complete rest from exercise. By limiting cardio to no more than five sessions per week, you will help regenerate your energy supplies and enhance recuperation. Remember, more is not necessarily better. Too much aerobic activity can cause your body to fuel your workout by breaking down muscle tissue. Ultimately, this will lead to a decrease in muscle tone and a slowdown of your metabolic system—the opposite effect of what you seek.

• *Duration:* As a rule, you should perform cardiovascular exercise for approximately 20 to 45 minutes per session. Although some studies indicate that you can obtain aerobic benefits after only 12 minutes of cardiovascular activity, it is generally necessary to perform a minimum of 20 minutes to accelerate the fat-burning process. Research has shown that it takes approximately 20 minutes of continuous aerobic exercise before fat is released from cells and becomes available as fuel. Therefore, if fat burning is your goal, consider 20 minutes of cardio a minimum. Alternatively, performing aerobics for protracted intervals produces diminishing returns. As with training too frequently, performing cardio for extended periods can easily lead to overtraining. To avoid this, I suggest that you spend no more than 45 minutes in an aerobic session. Unless you are training for a marathon, 45 minutes is enough to ensure maximum benefits without risk.

• *Intensity:* Although there are many ways to measure aerobic intensity, one of the easiest and most effective methods is by maximal heart rate (220 minus your age). Using this method, you should perform cardiovascular exercise at a stable pulse of 50 to 90 percent of your maximal heart rate. Be sure to begin with a brief warm-up at low intensity and finish with a cool-down at a similar level. As you progress in your training endeavors, you should attempt to elevate the intensity of your aerobic sessions until you are training at close to 80 percent of your maximal heart rate. Not only does this allow you to accomplish more in less time, it also helps condition your cardiovascular system to deliver oxygen efficiently to your muscles. This, in turn, will increase the endurance capability of your working muscles. Although you will be performing weight training at a rapid pace, efficient oxygen transfer is crucial in your efforts to push through a set. When training in a high-energy format, poor cardiovascular capacity will diminish your ability to endure a complete weight-training session.

• *Variation:* As with the weight-training component of this system, you should vary your aerobic routine, cross-training among at least three different aerobic modalities (bike, treadmill, stairmaster, and so forth). Cross-training, an essential concept in aerobic training, helps reduce boredom and promotes adherence to your routine. You can best accomplish cross-training by alternating modalities from one workout to the next, never allowing your body to become accustomed to a particular exercise. In this way, you keep your body off guard, preventing specific adaptation. Moreover, because you use different muscles in exercise performance, you do not subject your bones, muscles, and joints to continual impact, significantly reducing the likelihood of injury. All told, cross-training should be an integral part of your cardiovascular regimen.

Cardiovascular Protocols

Duration:	20 to 45 minutes per session
Frequency:	3 to 5 days a week
Intensity:	50 to 80% of maximal heart rate
Variation:	Alternate among 3 or 4 exercise modalities

The element in the margin summarizes the High-Energy Fitness protocols for cardiovascular training. As with weight training, proper manipulation of these protocols will determine how far you will go in your efforts. Because your aerobic routine will affect your weight-training program, striking the right balance between the two is essential in optimizing your physique. I advise you to proceed cautiously here, starting with the minimum recommended levels and advancing with care. Although the usual inclination is to go all out, you run the risk of pushing too far. There is a fine line between training and overtraining, and only prudence will prevent you from crossing it.

Now that you know how to incorporate aerobics appropriately into your routine, you face another dilemma: which specific exercises should you perform for best results? Fitness experts have hotly debated this issue, and many have proposed one exercise as the best. Such a wide range of modalities is available that the consumer is overwhelmed with options. Making matters worse, new types of cardiovascular machines are continually flooding the market. Marketers use fancy infomercials to promote these machines, often hiring a celebrity to claim that theirs is the "ultimate fat-burning vehicle." With all the hype surrounding these machines, how do you separate fact from fiction?

In truth, when all factors are considered, there is not much difference in total calories burned among most of these modalities. Table 15.1 lists the approximate caloric expenditure for some of the more common aerobic activities. Note that the figures listed are for calories burned per hour. If you were to perform an activity for a half hour, a more reasonable duration, the discrepancy between exercises would be even less significant.

At first glance, it would seem that the treadmill would be the exercise of choice for aerobic performance. After all, it burns the most calories of all the modalities. These figures, however, do not take into account the body's propensity for adaptation, which greatly influences caloric expenditure. As previously noted, the human body readily adjusts to external stimuli by becoming more proficient in the activity, continually improving its efficiency. The only way to counteract this is by continually increasing the intensity of the activity—a course that has a

Table 15.1 Caloric Expenditure for Selected Aerobic Activities

ACTIVITY	CALORIES PER HOUR	
	Moderate	Vigorous
Bike with arms	255	355
Cross-country ski machine	298	339
Rowing machine	303	370
Stairmaster	314	373
Stationary bike	249	302
Treadmill	353	433

Enjoy the treadmill if you like, but avoid using it exclusively.

limited ceiling. Hence, using the treadmill exclusively will inevitably lead to diminished returns. As detailed in the variation protocol, cross-training among exercises is the only way to avoid this phenomenon, and it therefore yields the best results. Despite the hype, there simply is no single best exercise! Using the treadmill, or any other modality, at the exclusion of other activities is counterproductive.

A good way to boost aerobic intensity is to incorporate rhythmic arm movements into the activity. When you swing your arms back and forth at shoulder level, your heart pumps blood against the force of gravity, increasing oxygen consumption and burning additional calories.

It is of interest to note that swimming is a poor choice as a fat burner. Although it can promote an excellent degree of cardiovascular fitness, swimming can actually add additional fat to your body. Because water temperature is well below your normal body temperature (unless you swim in a hot tub), swimming causes your body to struggle to preserve its internal heat. Over time, your body responds by developing an insulating layer of fat. This defense mechanism is not conducive to maintaining a lean physique. Therefore, from a bodysculpting perspective, swimming should be enjoyed only on an occasional basis.

Another often-asked question concerns the timing of cardiovascular exercise: should it be done at the beginning or at the end of your workout? Many women like to perform aerobics when they first get to the gym, while others prefer to wait until they have finished training with weights. Although there is no definitive answer to this query, a good case can be made for performing your cardio after your weight-training session. Several benefits substantiate this line of reasoning.

First, aerobics help flush metabolic waste from your body. These unwanted by-products from muscular overload are a hindrance to your bodysculpting aspirations. After a high-energy weight-training session, a great deal of waste, particularly lactic acid, accrues within your muscles. Performing cardio after lifting can help remove this undesired waste, enhancing recuperation and speeding recovery.

Second, because weight training requires much higher intensity than aerobics, you need more energy for exercise performance. By training with weights when your energy reserves are high, you can go all out in your lifting efforts. As energy levels dissipate, your weight-training ability wanes and your capacity to train effectively is compromised. Alternatively, because cardio requires less than all-out intensity, the timing of performance is of less consequence. Within reason, your aerobic ability should not be substantially affected by when you perform it.

Finally, if you become fatigued or are pressed for time, you can postpone your cardio routine without repercussions. Your body can regenerate much more quickly from aerobics than from weight training, allowing you greater flexibility with the timing of your cardiovascular regimen. As long as you get in a prescribed number of workouts per week, the structure by which you execute the routine is of little consequence. Because you can do cardio several days in a row, you have the luxury of deviating from your regular schedule to accommodate your immediate desires.

Although these factors suggest it is more beneficial to save cardio until the end of your workout, the overall impact is normally not that great. If you have good cardiovascular capacity, you can achieve results either way. I recommend that you experiment with both methods and assess the effect on your workouts. Listen to your body and then make your determination on this issue. If you are more comfortable performing your cardio first, then of course, go for it!

Finally, as in all facets of exercise, training in a safe climate is of paramount importance when structuring your aerobic routine. Many potential pitfalls are associated with aerobics, and avoiding them is critical for you to remain injury free. Because women are especially prone to joint-related ailments, this consideration becomes even more consequential.

One particular area of concern involves aerobics classes. As recommended earlier, you should, for the most part, avoid them. These classes are not only inferior in their ability to burn calories but also dramatically heighten the potential for injury. Accordingly, use cardiovascular machines such as the treadmill, stationary bike, stair climber, and so on whenever possible. From an overall perspective, they provide an excellent risk-reward combination and are the modalities of choice for aerobic training.

Running presents another potential aerobic hazard. More than any type of cardio, running can have a debilitating effect on your shins and knees. Studies have shown that frequent runners have up to a 70 percent rate of injury to the lower extremities. These results are magnified when you run on the street or on a paved surface, which exacerbates stress on the joints. Moreover, obstacles such as potholes, wet leaves, and snow can cause undue torque on the knee joint, creating the potential for serious injury.

If you do choose to run or jog, I recommend that you do so on a high-quality treadmill. A treadmill has a cushioned surface that absorbs some of the stress on your shins and knees. Although this does not completely relieve these shearing forces, the impact is somewhat softened. As a side benefit, the treadmill forces you to regulate your speed, keeping your heart rate constant. If you simply cannot resist running outdoors, do so on a track specifically designed for this purpose. In addition, consider wearing a knee brace for extra support and stabilization. Your legs will thank you!

You must also be careful to maintain your aerobic focus. As opposed to weight training, cardio tends to promote injuries of indiscretion. Because you perform weight training for brief intervals at high intensity, you must focus on the activity at hand. A set lasts only a minute, and it is easy to maintain your concentration throughout the lift. On the other hand, aerobic sessions can go on for extended periods, and letting your mind wander can help pass the time. But this can encourage sloppiness in training, increasing the chance of injury. Be smart: pay attention to your form and don't become careless!

16 Safe Workouts During Pregnancy

Pregnancy can be one of the most exhilarating experiences known to a woman, but its effects on the body can also make it one of the most demoralizing. As a personal trainer, I often hear from women who have had babies that they cannot lose their pregnancy weight after giving birth. During pregnancy, women undergo many physiologic and hormonal changes that can drastically alter their metabolism and physical condition. For a woman who has been in peak condition, this can wreak havoc on her self-esteem.

Unfortunately, many women still believe that pregnancy requires a sedentary lifestyle. Fearing that strenuous activity will threaten their well-being, they become couch potatoes. Even worse, some train haphazardly while pregnant, jeopardizing not only their health but that of their fetus as well. There are so many misconceptions about training during pregnancy that many obstetricians are not sure how to counsel their patients on this subject. Yet a properly implemented exercise regimen can provide many positive effects for the pregnant woman, with virtually no downside. You can derive the following benefits from a well-executed training routine:

• *Exercise decreases the risk of postpartum obesity.* Although it is certainly possible to reshape your body after pregnancy, the best way to counteract postpartum weight is to stay in shape *during* pregnancy. By dedicating yourself to a regimented workout schedule, you can return to virtually your original shape shortly

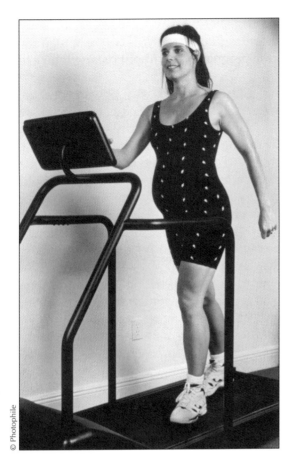

© Photophile

Exercise during pregnancy makes it easier to lose excess weight after delivery.

after childbirth. Training allows you to preserve muscle mass throughout the term, keeping your resting metabolic rate elevated. Because your overall activity level tends to decrease during this period, sustaining your metabolism is important. This will hinder excessive weight gain and make weight loss easier after delivery.

• *Exercise improves physical and mental well-being during pregnancy.* Pregnant women who remain active are less likely to lose their motivation and self-confidence. Training increases your energy level, reduces fatigue, and promotes a better sense of well-being. This, in turn, boosts self-esteem, so you can fully enjoy this period of your life.

• *Exercise reduces the incidence of lower-back pain and related ailments.* Lower-back problems are one of the most common ailments experienced during pregnancy. Because a woman carries an extra 20 pounds or more in her abdominal region, a structural imbalance is created that places a great deal of stress on the lower back. If the muscles in this area are weak, stress is heightened, increasing the probability of developing lower-back pain. Exercise strengthens this region, improving posture and preventing potential problems. By maintaining muscular health, you can prevent many related anomalies, thus preserving your physical well-being.

• *Exercise may provide for an easier labor.* One of a woman's worst fears during pregnancy is the thought of enduring a grueling, prolonged labor. Research suggests that continued exercise, particularly throughout late pregnancy, may have a positive effect on the course of labor. The increased strength and level of fitness acquired through a regimented exercise program improves placental growth and function, regulating contractions and facilitating a smooth delivery. Overall, the entire childbirth process is greatly enhanced, diminishing the pain and discomfort associated with labor.

Of course, common sense should prevail before you undertake an exercise regimen. If you have been sedentary before conception, you will need to work into a program at a much slower pace than a woman who is physically fit. If you have never trained before, now is not the time to get bold.

Regardless of your level of fitness, a pregnancy workout will take longer than usual. You must do everything at a deliberate, leisurely pace. To prepare your body adequately, spend extra time in the warm-up. Proceed through your routine with caution, taking as much time as necessary to keep your heart rate at acceptable levels.

To derive proper benefits, you must understand the unique nuances of working out during pregnancy. When pregnant, your response to physical activity changes substantially. You simply cannot train at high-energy levels and must restrict some of your actions and motions for the sake of your baby's health. Your fitness goal during this period is not to optimize your physique but to maintain a high level of fitness consistent with maximum safety. By following certain basic guidelines and remaining diligent in the pursuit of your goals, you can reap the rewards of staying fit during and after the pregnancy—without risking injury to yourself or the fetus.

Before beginning a routine, you should first consult with your physician to rule out any possible contraindications for exercise. Conditions such as hypertension, bleeding, cardiac arrhythmia, and other afflictions are potentially injurious. Even things that might seem innocuous under normal circumstances can become acute during the physical changes of pregnancy. Therefore, medical clearance is a necessary prerequisite before undertaking a training regimen, and you should obtain regular follow-up to monitor changes in your health. In this case, an ounce of prevention really is worth a pound of cure.

If no unusual circumstances exist, you are ready to begin training. The structure of your workout will remain largely the same as in the body-conditioning phase of this system, with adjustments made based on the physical constraints of pregnancy. You will again employ a combination of stretching, weight training, and cardiovascular exercise, with set and rep schemes similar to those outlined earlier. You should plan to exercise at regular intervals using the same three-day-per-week training schedule advocated throughout this book (for example, Monday, Wednesday, Friday). Adequate rest is particularly important at this time, and you must listen to your body. Accordingly, if you feel at all fatigued, allow an additional day or two of recuperation.

A consideration vital to prenatal health is maintaining stable body temperature while training. Some research suggests that pregnancy increases your basal metabolic temperature, predisposing your body to overheating (a condition called hyperthermia). Exercising in a hot, humid place makes it difficult for your body to cool itself, substantially increasing the risk of heat-related illness. Thus, you must make sure that your training facility is well ventilated and air conditioned, allowing your body to remain cool throughout the workout. In addition, you should wear loose clothing to provide adequate ventilation and dissipation of body heat. Dress appropriately when you work out: supportive shoes to maintain balance, a maternity bra with lots of support, and temperature-appropriate clothes (tights and layers in cold temperatures, cotton T-shirts and shorts in warm temperatures). Monitor your body temperature throughout your workout. If you notice any sharp variances, stop training immediately.

It is also important to remain well hydrated throughout your workout. Severe dehydration can lead to heat exhaustion or even heat stroke—with potentially disastrous consequences. Chronic dehydration can lead to premature labor. You should consume up to a pint of liquid before exercise and a minimum of one cup for every 20 minutes of training. This will ensure adequate fluid replacement to replenish fluid lost through perspiration. A final warning: do not use thirst as a measure of hydration. By the time you're thirsty, your body is already becoming dehydrated.

As always, begin your workout with a warm-up. This is especially important during pregnancy. Hormonal changes associated with pregnancy cause a softening of your connective tissue. This, in turn, relaxes your ligaments, making them unstable and susceptible to injury. A proper warm-up helps circulate blood throughout your body, alleviating stress in the joints and thereby decreasing the risk of impairment. Use a program similar to the one in chapter 2, taking extra time to ensure that your body is thoroughly warm. To reduce risk further, never stretch

Remain well hydrated during exercise by consuming plenty of water.

to the point of maximum resistance. Instead, perform stretches in a relaxed manner that stays within a comfortable zone. Of course, you should avoid any ballistic, bouncing movements, which are especially hazardous at this time.

Next, you should move on to a structured weight-training regimen. It is unfortunate that many women abandon weight-bearing exercise at the onset of pregnancy. There is a mistaken belief that weight training is too dangerous during pregnancy, with limited benefits because of physical restrictions. But as long as you follow established protocols, weight training poses little risk. When properly implemented, it is one of the safest training alternatives available. Moreover, weight training is the only modality that allows you to preserve lean muscle tissue, preventing your metabolism from slowing to a crawl. If you want to stay in shape during term, do not omit this essential component from your workout.

As in the body-conditioning phase, use a total-body workout as the foundation of your routine. This directs blood flow into all areas of the body, ensuring adequate circulation to the fetus throughout your routine. Moreover, each muscle group continually receives direct stimulus, helping to maintain overall fitness levels.

You must, however, substantially modify this process to accommodate the demands of pregnancy. There are many distinct contraindications to exercise, and anything that might jeopardize the pregnancy is explicitly taboo. Although the outline of this workout will be familiar, strictly observe the following protocols, with attention to maternal symptoms:

• *Exercises:* Use only one exercise per muscle group, training your entire body during each workout. It is still beneficial to vary your exercises, making sure to avoid the contraindications covered later in this chapter. Remember your focus is on maintaining your fitness level, not on bodysculpting. Employing advanced training techniques will therefore be of little benefit. Instead, keep your workout simple and concentrate on basic movements. Discard from your routine any exercise that you find uncomfortable to perform, substituting movements more conducive to your present status.

• *Sets:* When pregnant, the number of sets that you perform will vary based on your energy reserves. At the onset of pregnancy, you should strive to perform three sets of each exercise, an ideal scheme for virtually all fitness goals. This will sufficiently stimulate your muscle fibers without overtraining your body. As your term progresses, adjust the volume of exercise according to your stamina. If you feel overtired toward the end of your workout, lighten the workload and pare down to two or even one set per exercise.

• *Rest:* The pace of a pregnancy routine will be decidedly slower than normal, using rest intervals of one minute or more between sets. Unlike high-energy workouts, weight training during pregnancy should not be an aerobic endeavor. Because pregnancy results in an increase in body weight and reduced oxygen efficiency, your body requires longer rest intervals to maintain strength and energy reserves. As a rule, allow your heart rate to return to near resting levels before beginning a new set. Still, you should avoid remaining stationary between sets, which can decrease your cardiac output and lead to cardiovascular symptoms. By simply walking around slowly during rest intervals, you maintain healthy circulation and avert decreasing blood flow.

• *Repetitions:* During pregnancy, it is especially important to use a high-repetition scheme in your routine. The target rep number can be as high as 25 per set, never lower than 15 reps unless you experience fatigue. Obviously, you are not training for strength or power, and using high reps is necessary to protect your joints and connective tissue from inflammation. Repetitions should be smooth and controlled, with particular emphasis on maintaining form. A variety of complications can arise should you swing or jerk up a weight while lifting. Use special care to work through a functional range of motion. Moreover, be sure to regulate your breathing on each rep, keeping it slow and rhythmic. Never hold your breath during a lift, which increases intra-abdominal pressure and heightens your risk of becoming dizzy or fainting.

• *Intensity:* You should perform all sets using a weight no more than 75 percent of your maximum poundage. Training too intensely during pregnancy can have disastrous ramifications. Use extreme caution in this regard. Your aim is to induce mild muscular stimulation, not strain your resources. Never should you struggle while lifting a weight. If a set becomes difficult, don't hesitate to stop short of completing it. Although you may tend to become caught up in the moment, you must use restraint when lifting, making sure not to push too hard. Training during pregnancy is not a high-energy endeavor! To ensure proper training pace, measure your maximal heart rate during peak activity and do not allow it to exceed 140 beats per minute.

The element in the margin summarizes the protocols for pregnancy training. I cannot overemphasize the importance of taking these protocols seriously. Pregnancy is a complex state with so many variables that there is little margin for error. On the other hand, it can be detrimental to be overcautious in your training philosophy. This can lead to a tentative approach that may result in injury. The best way to train is to understand all the variables, stay relaxed, and train within your limitations.

As indicated earlier, many exercises are contraindicated during pregnancy. Because of the physiologic and hormonal changes that occur, certain movements are potentially harmful not only to yourself but to your fetus. To avoid possible conflicts, you should understand the theory behind these contraindications. This will allow you to determine whether an exercise is safe based on the execution of the movement.

Pregnancy Training Protocols

Exercises:	1 per muscle group
Sets:	3 per exercise
Rest:	1 minute or more between sets
Repetitions:	15 to 20 per set
Intensity:	75% or less of maximum

• *Avoid exercises that incorporate bending from the waist.* Because of the uneven weight distribution in pregnancy, bending can be uncomfortable. During exercise, movements that require bending can lead to a variety of complications including dizziness and heartburn. Moreover, they tend to place undue stress on the lumbar spine, possibly causing injury to the lower back. These can be precursors to other, more serious anomalies. Thus, you should not perform exercises such as stiff-legged deadlifts and bent rows after the first several months of pregnancy. As a substitute, you can use modified positions such as elbows and knees or all fours to target the gluteal and hamstring area. If necessary, you can facilitate these movements with towels or pillows to maintain proper body alignment.

• *Abandon all overhead lifting exercises.* Although exercise can strengthen the muscles of the lower back, you must use extreme caution in this area during pregnancy. As previously noted, lower-back pain is one of the most common ailments experienced by pregnant women. Because of postural changes, overhead exercises tend to increase pressure on the lower back, making this area vulnerable to injury. As the term progresses, structural imbalances are magnified. Thus, you should not use exercises such as the military press and incline chest press.

• *Abandon exercises performed in the supine position after the first trimester.* Because of the redistribution of circulatory flow, pregnant women are prone to decreased blood pressure (hypotension). Exercises performed in the supine position can exacerbate this condition, causing a woman to become light headed and dizzy. Furthermore, these exercises allow the fetus to press on the vena cava, decreasing blood flow to the fetus. When circulation is obstructed, oxygen supply to the fetus is reduced, which can cause dire complications. Thus, omit exercises such as the bench press, crunch, lying triceps extensions, and so forth after the third month of term.

Although these restrictions will limit your training alternatives, you still have many exercises from which to choose. Table 16.1 shows a sample weight-training routine that incorporates the principles discussed above and demonstrates the potential for adding variety and interest to your program. If you are creative, you will find a myriad of possibilities at your disposal.

Table 16.1   Sample Three-Day Pregnancy Weight-Training Program

Muscle group	Day 1	Day 2	Day 3
Chest	Seated rows	Straight-arm pulldowns	Dumbbell rows
Back	Lateral raises	Upright rows	Front raises
Shoulders	Pec decks	Cable crossovers	Modified push-ups
Biceps	Seated dumbbell curls	EZ curls	Cable curls
Triceps	Pushdowns	Kickbacks	Overhead extensions
Quadriceps	Leg extensions	Lunges	Seated leg presses
Hamstrings and glutes	Standing leg curls	Abductor pulls	Floor kicks
Calves	Seated calf raises	Standing calf raises	Toe presses
Abdominals	Knee-ins	Bench leg raises	Side bends

Cap your workout with a period of cardiovascular activity. Here, too, safety is a critical issue, and you must observe several restrictions. Limit your aerobic activity to 20 minutes. Your heart rate should not exceed 70 percent of your age-related maximum. A good way to monitor your intensity is to use a technique called the talk test. The talk test simply requires that you be able to speak in complete sentences without gasping for breath. If you are unable to carry on a conversation, the work rate is too hard and you should reduce your level of effort. Although the talk test errs on the side of caution, it keeps you focused on maintaining a stable pulse and helps ensure an acceptable training intensity.

I do not recommend aerobics classes, especially high-impact and step, during pregnancy. I have already discussed the drawbacks of these classes, which are of even greater concern during this period. Because of the aforementioned joint instability associated with pregnancy, you are particularly vulnerable to stressful activities. The bouncing movements, jumping motions, and rapid directional changes inherent to aerobics classes exert heavy stress on the body, often causing strains, sprains, or even fractures of the extremities. Moreover, because postural changes of pregnancy distort your equilibrium, you may find it difficult to maintain balance while performing movements in these classes. This can lead to slips or falls—a dangerous prospect at this time.

For the cardiovascular component of your workout, it is best to adhere to a routine that uses individual activities. Exercises such as the treadmill, stationary bike, and stairmaster are fine choices for your routine. These modalities allow you to remain in control during exercise and are flexible enough that you can adapt them to your abilities. Using these modalities will ensure a high degree of safety and produce optimal results.

Complete your workout with a relaxing stretching routine.

After cardio, it is best to finish the workout with gentle stretching movements, following the principles you used in the warm-up. This will gradually stabilize your body temperature and help flush lactic acid from your working muscles. Stretch for as long as you desire, making sure you have completely cooled down before leaving the gym.

If no complications arise during your pregnancy, you can continue with this program nearly until term. As long as you have the energy and motivation, there is no risk in training up to delivery. Although you may want to reduce the frequency or length of your sessions, your routine can continue as described without ill effect. The numerous benefits of exercise make it advantageous to continue with your program as long as you can.

After childbirth, you should normally be able to return to your training regimen within three to four weeks. Again, check with your physician before restarting your training program. When you return, you should begin as if you were starting from scratch. Because many of the physiologic and morphologic changes of pregnancy persist for up to six weeks after delivery, you should resume training gradually. Consider yourself a beginner again and follow the protocols outlined in the body conditioning routine (see chapter 3). With diligence, you will quickly achieve your previous level of fitness.

That's it, a comprehensive routine that is safe and effective! Your entire pregnancy workout will last about an hour to an hour and a half and should leave you feeling healthy and invigorated. By following the principles and dedicating yourself to a regimented workout schedule, you can maintain your shape throughout pregnancy and ultimately look as good as or better than you did before conception!

17 Maintaining Your Physique

Your journey to physique heaven is almost complete. After training in the advanced phase of this system, the world of bodysculpting is now your oyster. You are the master of your physique, in complete control of your destiny—what a powerful feeling! You are now at a crossroads in your training endeavors and must decide which route you want to take.

Before determining a course of action, you must evaluate your options and match them with your training goals. Even at advanced levels, training is a dynamic process that demands constant attention to detail. To make an intelligent decision when going forward, you must know where you are and in what direction you want to go. Accordingly, the following are some of the issues to contemplate: Are you satisfied with your present condition? Do you always want to be in your best shape? Are you prepared to continue training at maximum intensity? How you answer these questions will dictate your training philosophy from here on out.

If you want to keep your hard-earned gains, there is no getting around the fact that you will need to keep up your fitness regimen. Exercise is a lifetime commitment that requires consistent participation to sustain a high degree of muscle tone. Although you may theorize that it will no longer be necessary to train once you attain your ideal physique, nothing could be further from the truth. You will have to train as hard as you did before, if not harder, if you intend to make continued aesthetic improvements to your body.

After working so diligently to perfect your physique, it would be a shame to see it deteriorate. But that is exactly what will happen if you stop working out. During such a period, called detraining, your muscles gradually start to atrophy (decrease in size), losing their hardness and density. Along with this loss of muscle tissue, your metabolism begins to slow down, causing a corresponding increase in body-fat storage. Over time, your physique will return to pretraining levels. Alas, you will look as if you had never worked out.

Fortunately, you can take heart in the fact that detraining does not take place overnight. Your body craves stability and will try to establish a comfort zone at a given set point (a phenomenon called homeostasis). Once your body establishes this set point, it attempts to maintain homeostasis by defending itself against any shift away from this state. Thus, if you have kept yourself in peak condition for a substantial time, your body will strive to stay in shape, using all its resources to avoid a loss of muscle tissue.

Although individual factors determine the actual rate of detraining, you will experience virtually no change in body composition from a brief layoff. On average, muscular atrophy is negligible for up to two weeks of inactivity. In fact, a short period of inactivity can be beneficial to your body, providing increased stamina for future workouts (if you have been training consistently for a substantial time). After two weeks, the effects of detraining will begin to become apparent. Still, you should notice only about a 10 percent decline in body composition after a month without training—a fairly insignificant amount. Even after a six-month hiatus, you can generally maintain as much as 50 percent of your gains, giving your body at least a semblance of muscle tone and definition.

Moreover, it is significantly easier to regain your shape after a layoff. Because of a phenomenon known as muscle memory, your body is sensitized to recover lost muscle tissue when you reintroduce training. Although there is no definitive scientific explanation for this curiosity, it is a fact that your body responds more rapidly to exercise the second time around. On average, you can expect to shape your ideal physique in roughly half the time it took previously.

Muscle and Fat

Fat cannot turn into muscle, and muscle cannot turn into fat—this is physiologically impossible. When you stop weight training, the muscle that you have developed will gradually atrophy (get smaller). After a given time, your muscles will eventually return to their starting point. Generally, the longer you have been training, the longer it will take for you to lose muscle tissue.

It is a common mistake to maintain caloric intake after the cessation of a weight-training program. Because muscle raises resting metabolic rate and allows the body to burn more calories, you will be able to consume more food when you are on a fitness program. When you stop training, however, you must reassess your eating habits and take in fewer calories to balance a slowdown in metabolism. If you don't cut back on your calorie intake, you will experience weight gain and see the illusion of your muscle turning into fat.

Although you should avoid detraining at all costs, it sometimes becomes inevitable. If, for any reason, you must undergo a prolonged period of inactivity (because of injury, family crisis, or other circumstance), you will need to reacclimate your muscles to the training process. Your initial reaction might be to jump back into your routine and make up for lost time, but you must resist this imprudent temptation. Once detraining has occurred, your body will have a reduced capacity for exertion. Although your mind might be willing to train all out, your body won't be able to handle that level of intensity. Attempting to do the work-

After a layoff from training, use longer rest intervals until your body readjusts.

out you were once accustomed to would cause severe trauma to your entire neuromuscular system, potentially leading to serious injury.

Accordingly, you should take a cautious approach upon your return. Because the extent of detraining is directly correlated to length of inactivity, you should progress at a pace consistent with the length of time you have been sedentary. This will ensure that you don't overtax your neuromuscular system and will help prevent a debilitating injury that could derail your comeback efforts.

In general, you need make only minor modifications to your routine if your layoff is less than three months in duration. In your first workout back, reduce training intensity to roughly 75 percent of your maximum. Rest slightly longer than normal, taking up to a minute between sets. It is best to avoid using any supersets or giant sets, concentrating solely on regaining your strength and endurance. Over the next several workouts, you can begin to increase intensity and reduce rest intervals, gradually working back to previous levels. Within a month, you can resume training in a high-energy format and should be close to recovering your prior condition.

On the other hand, if your layoff extends more than three months, it is generally best to start from the beginning. You will need to reestablish your motor skills and rebuild a foundation of muscle. To accomplish this objective, you should use the body-conditioning phase of this system, training your entire body each workout (see chapter 3).

During your first few weeks, make sure to take things in a slow, deliberate fashion. Your focus should be on regenerating the neuromuscular pathways necessary for optimal performance. It will take some time to get back into a training groove, and you must be patient in your efforts. Once you have accomplished these objectives, you should continue through the system in a stepwise fashion. With diligence, you will be able to make rapid progress, returning to your previous best within a few months.

If you are willing and able to keep up your fitness regimen (and have not experienced a long layoff), you now must decide whether you want to actualize your full potential or simply maintain your present body composition. If you are content with your level of development or no longer wish to train with all-out intensity, then maintenance is a viable option.

But don't expect the maintenance routine to be a walk in the park. You cannot simply go through the motions and expect to retain your proportions magically. On the contrary, if you slack off for a prolonged period, a gradual degradation of your muscle tissue will take place. Although this decline will not be as severe as if you discontinued training altogether (any stimulus is better than none), a prolonged period of reduced effort will certainly degrade the quality of your

Carol Semple-Marzetta: Ms. Fitness Olympia

Height: 5'6"

Weight: 125

400 Corporate Circle Unit M, Golden, CO 80401

Photo courtesy of Carol Semple-Marzetta

An injury can be an obstacle to developing your physique. No one knows this better than Carol. She longed to be a professional gymnast and was one of the most accomplished athletes in Colorado. Then, at the end of her junior year in high school, a serious car crash abruptly ended her gymnastic aspirations.

Carol damaged the tendons, ligaments, and muscles in her lower back. After months of physical therapy, Carol set out to strengthen and rejuvenate her body. "I was always fascinated with the human body and how it works. So, at the end of school, I took the summer off and learned as much as I could about exercise physiology and kinesiology. I spoke to anyone who appeared knowledgeable about weight training and researched many journals on the topic. Gradually, I developed a base of information that allowed me to create a successful training routine."

"When you're training around an injury, it's imperative to train smart and listen to your body. You need to distinguish between when your body tells you it needs a break from when your mind tells you it needs a break. Early on, I learned this distinction and was able to sense when I was pushing it too much."

Carol makes sure to lift with proper form and also pays strict attention to the types of moves in her routine. "There are several exercises that are extremely dangerous for those with lower back problems. For example, I won't do squats, bent rows, or any exercise performed in the standing position. Whenever possible, I try to choose movements where my back is fully supported, and I can go to failure without worrying about hurting myself."

Carol also emphasizes the importance of abdominal training in rehabilitating lower back injuries. "The abs play an integral role in lower back function. Strengthening them is one of the best things you can do to promote a healthy lower back. With my history of injury, I've always been especially conscious of achieving complete abdominal development."

Carol is a testament to what can be achieved through intelligent effort. "Without a doubt, I attribute my success in fitness to training in a scientific fashion. Despite my limitations, I was able to overcome a dreadful injury and make it to the top of the sport."

Carol's training tip

"Fitness isn't a quick fix—it's a lifelong commitment. With proper diligence, you'll enjoy the benefits that it affords forever."

physique. Unless you will be satisfied with losing some of your hard-earned gains, you must be willing to exert maximal effort at least occasionally.

To maintain your physique at optimal levels, you will be best served by using a concept called periodization. Simply stated, periodization (sometimes referred to as cycling) is a structured way to vary your workouts at regular time intervals. You do this by altering one or more training variables in a progressive format to attain a variety of training goals.

Bodybuilders often use a periodized program to peak for a competition, structuring their routines into heavy, medium, and light cycles. For instance, a periodized bodybuilding routine normally begins with a heavy cycle. During this phase, the bodybuilder trains for strength and size, trying to pack on as much muscle as possible. Next, the bodybuilder uses a medium cycle, honing the muscle developed earlier into aesthetic proportion. Finally, the competitor employs a light cycle, attempting to bring out maximum detail in each muscle and strip away all excess body fat. Properly executed, this routine will mold strength, size, and definition into perfect symmetry—creating a classic bodybuilding physique.

Although periodization is most commonly associated with power lifting and bodybuilding, it can be modified to work beautifully as a maintenance strategy for women. Because your body strives to preserve homeostasis, you can retain a high degree of muscle tone with only sporadic bouts of all-out training. By employing alternating cycles of maximal and submaximal effort, you will exert enough neuromuscular stimuli to retain your shape, while being able to enjoy periods of carefree training.

In the maintenance program, you will continue to use the targeted body-sculpting phase of this system while compartmentalizing your routine into three distinct cycles—low intensity, medium intensity, and high intensity. You will perform each cycle for a month, repeating the procedure at the end of the third month. You will keep all other training variables constant, including high reps and brief rest intervals. This will ensure that you preserve your aerobic conditioning and metabolic state, minimizing any gain in body fat. For best results, follow these protocols:

- *Month 1 (low-intensity cycle):* During this cycle, you should perform training at approximately 70 to 75 percent of maximum intensity. The objective of this phase is to preserve a basic level of conditioning and prohibit a tangible loss of muscle tone. You should focus on keeping a quick pace to your routine, moving freely from one movement to the next. There is no need to struggle at this point, since muscular failure is not the goal. Although this phase will produce a mild aerobic effect, it will not tax your resources nor will it cause significant muscular fatigue. If you truly loathe the muscular pain associated with high-energy training, you should enjoy this phase of your workout!

- *Month 2 (moderate-intensity cycle):* During this cycle, you perform training at approximately 85 to 90 percent of maximum intensity. The objective of this phase is to bridge your transition back to high-energy levels, preparing your body for all-out training. Your workouts will now require more physical exertion, and you should feel reasonably fatigued by the end of your session. Although you will not be training to failure, the last few reps of a set should be somewhat of a struggle. Still, this phase won't produce the severe muscular discomfort associated with high-energy training.

High-energy training means going all out!

• *Month 3 (high-intensity cycle):* During this cycle, you should perform training at 100 percent intensity, taking each set to momentary muscular failure. The objective here is to shock your system, actively stimulating all your muscle fibers. You will now be training in a true high-energy format, with the intention of pushing yourself to the limit. This is the most important phase of the maintenance cycle because it fully taxes your resources and forces your body to maintain homeostasis at elite levels. Unless you go all out in your efforts, you will not stress your body enough to keep your hard-earned gains.

Let me warn you that you must deal with some psychological ramifications of working a maintenance program. During the low-intensity cycles, it is quite common to feel as though you are out of shape. "I feel soft and flabby," is a frequent lament during these periods. These feelings, however, are largely perceptual. As previously stated, once you have developed a high degree of muscular conditioning, detraining does not occur this rapidly. Although a slight degradation in your body composition is inevitable when you decrease training intensity, you will quickly regenerate any loss of muscle in your high-intensity cycle.

Maintenance training, however, is not for everyone. Although many women are content when they attain a certain level of development, others are never satisfied no matter how far they progress. If you possess a drive that compels you to be your best, then you won't be content using a maintenance program. Rather, you will need to train in a fashion conducive to the ongoing pursuit of physical perfection.

Unfortunately, the closer you have come to your potential, the harder it will be to make tangible improvements in your physique. Remember that you achieve muscle tone and definition through your body's response to intense neuromuscular stress. This response is your body's defense mechanism to prepare for its next encounter with a neuromuscular stimulus.

As you move along the path toward physique heaven, you will experience diminishing returns from your efforts. Your body begins to adapt to the intense stress of exercise and becomes less inclined to respond to a training stimulus. Moreover, because you are in much better physical condition, any enhancement of body composition will be more subtle in appearance. Correspondingly, the closer you come to actualizing your potential, the less room you have for improvement.

No one, however, can achieve physical perfection. Regardless of your level of development, there will forever be areas of your physique that can be worked on. You will become a physique connoisseur, seeking to tighten, shape, or tone certain body parts. Fortunately, you will always be able to make alterations to your physique, providing you are willing to put in the effort.

To make these improvements, you must continually force your body to adapt to the stresses of exercise. You can accomplish this only by constantly keeping your body off guard, never allowing it to adjust to your training regimen. You will need to use all your training knowledge to manipulate your routine for optimal effect. For instance, you can employ different bodysculpting techniques, alter the split of your routine, use different exercise equipment—do whatever you have to do to confuse your body and compel it to respond.

Mental focus is especially important here. Your mind can push your body to do things you may have never imagined, allowing you to soar to incredible heights. Harnessing all your mental capacity is crucial to working past the pain threshold—a limiting factor in aesthetic development. Mental strength will allow you to elevate your training intensity repeatedly, taxing your body in a manner necessary to make ongoing improvements.

One of the biggest mistakes you can make at advanced levels is becoming caught up in a train-at-all-costs mentality. After years of working out, training often turns into a ritual. It can become like a drug, taking over your mind, body, and soul. Many psychological motivations perpetuate this obsession. Perhaps you crave the special feeling of having a great body and feel out of shape after missing a workout. Perhaps you have built a social network and don't want to miss seeing your friends. Or perhaps you use your workout as a means of escaping the problems of everyday life and feel stressed out when you don't train. These and other factors can exert a powerful influence that compels you to go to the gym.

In extreme cases, a training addiction can become so severe that it causes you to experience withdrawal symptoms when you miss even a single training session. Frequently, this will result in a severe case of overtraining. Throughout this book, I have repeatedly preached about the deleterious effects that overtraining can have on your body. It will not only prohibit you from making further gains but begin to catabolize your muscle tissue.

Although a three-day-per-week regimen is generally sufficient for adequate recuperation, you will sometimes need additional rest. The demands of intense training combined with external factors (such as sleeping patterns, stress levels, or nutritional deficiencies) can sometimes overwhelm your body and weaken your immune function, making necessary an extra day or two of rest. This is especially true at advanced levels, where the ravages of sustained high-energy training begin to take a toll on your body. Therefore, you must always be in tune with your overall sense of being; if you feel weak or depleted and need an extra day off, take it! If you can't train at sufficient intensity, it is better to rest a day and come back stronger the next.

Avoid being blinded by emotion, ignoring your body's telltale signs. Although it is natural to feel that adding more sets or training more frequently will result in better gains, this most often is counterproductive. Don't lose sight of the fact that recuperation, not the act of training, is what produces gains in muscle tone. For optimal results, be dispassionate in your approach and train scientifically, not haphazardly.

Finally, no discussion of bodysculpting would be complete without mentioning the importance of nutrition. Nutrition is a complex subject that is beyond the scope of this book. A brief summary cannot do proper justice to the intricacies of this topic.

Without a sensible nutritional regimen, you will never maximize your genetic potential. Nutrition is at least as important as training in achieving your ideal physique, maybe more so. It is essential in regulating body-fat storage and in aiding the growth and repair of muscle tissue. I encourage you to learn as much as you can about nutrition and develop a consistent regimen that works for you.

I hope this book has inspired you to take control of your body and maximize your genetic potential. Whatever your bodysculpting goals may be, you now have the knowledge to be your best. Knowledge is power, giving you the ability to soar to extraordinary heights. By embracing a fitness lifestyle, you will be sound in mind and body. Be patient and persistent and you, like thousands of women, will change your life forever.

I'll see you in physique heaven!

Glossary

aerobic exercise: Any activity that allows the body to replenish oxygen to working muscles continuously. This endurance exercise is performed at low to moderate intensity. Aerobic exercise burns both fat and glycogen for fuel.

anaerobic exercise: Any activity that uses oxygen at a faster rate than the body can replenish it in the working muscles. By nature, this type of exercise is intense and short in duration. ATP and glycogen are the primary fuel sources.

barbell: A long bar, usually about 6 feet in length, that can accommodate weighted plates on each end. The Olympic barbell, which weighs 45 pounds, is the industry standard.

bench: An apparatus designed for performing exercises in a seated or lying position. Many benches are adjustable so that exercises can be performed at various angles.

bodysculpting: The art of shaping muscles to optimal proportions.

circuit training: A series of exercise machines set up in sequence. The exercises are performed one after the other, each stressing a different muscle group.

collar: A clamp that secures weighted plates on a barbell or dumbbell.

compound movement: An exercise that involves two or more joints in the performance of the movement. Examples include squats, bench presses, and chins.

contraction: The act of shortening a muscle.

definition: The absence of fat in the presence of well-developed muscle.

dumbbell: A shortened version of a barbell, usually about 12 inches in length, that allows an exercise to be performed one arm at a time.

exercise: An individual movement intended to tax muscular function.

EZ-curl bar: A specially configured barbell that has curves in the middle, intended to alleviate strain on the wrists.

failure: The point in an exercise where the trainee cannot physically perform another rep.

flexibility: A litheness of the joints, muscle, and connective tissue that dictates range of motion.

form: The technique used in performing the biomechanics of an exercise.

free weights: Barbells and dumbbells. Exercise machines are the alternative.

giant set: A series of three or more exercises performed in succession with no rest between sets.

hypertrophy: An increase in muscle mass.

intensity: The amount of effort involved in a set.

isolation movement: An exercise that involves only one joint in the performance of the movement. Examples include cable crossovers, biceps curls, and leg extensions.

Nautilus: A brand of exercise equipment found in many health clubs. The term has become synonymous with any exercise machine.

plates: Flat, round weights that can be placed at the end of a barbell or dumbbell.

pump: The pooling of blood in a muscle due to intense anaerobic exercise.

repetition (rep): One complete movement of an exercise.

resistance: The amount of weight used in an exercise.

rest interval: The amount of time taken between sets.

routine: The configuration of exercises, sets, and reps used in a training session.

set: A series of repetitions performed in succession.

superset: Two exercises performed in succession with no rest between sets.

symmetry: The way in which muscle groups complement one another, creating a proportional physique.

testosterone: A hormone that is responsible for promoting muscle mass.

About the Author

Brad Schoenfeld, Certified Personal Trainer, is a renowned expert on fitness and sports nutrition. As the owner/operator of the exclusive Personal Training Center for Women in Scarsdale, New York, he is regarded as one of the leading authorities on women's fitness. He is also a lifetime drug-free bodybuilder and has won numerous natural bodybuilding titles including the ANPPC Tri-State Naturals and USA Mixed Pairs crowns.

Schoenfeld is a popular freelance writer on a variety of fitness topics and is a regular contributor to many leading fitness magazines, including being a columnist and feature writer for *Fitness Magazine*. He has published numerous articles appearing in such magazines as *Shape, Let's Live, Muscle and Fitness, New Living, Martial Arts Training, Senior Magazine, Ms. Fitness, Natural Bodybuilding, Oxygen*, and *MuscleMag*. Moreover, he has been featured on television's CBS Evening News, CNN Headline News, and FOX Good Day New York, as well as on radio programs across the country.

Certified by the American Council on Exercise (ACE) and the Aerobics and Fitness Association of America (AFAA), Schoenfeld is President of Global Fitness Services, a diverse, multifaceted fitness corporation. Schoenfeld lives in Croton, New York. He may be contacted care of Global Fitness Services, Box 58, Scarsdale, NY 10583.

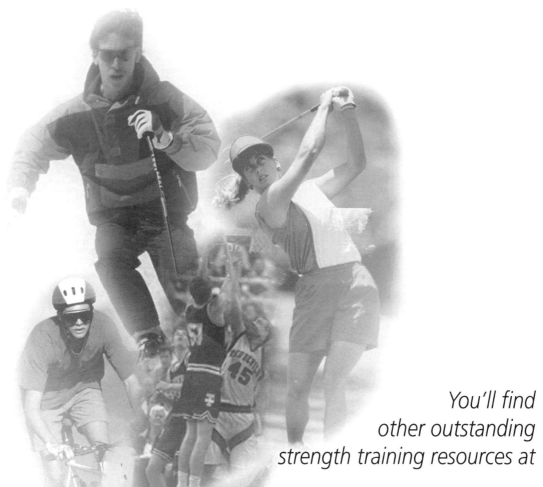

*You'll find
other outstanding
strength training resources at*

www.humankinetics.com

In the U.S. call

1-800-747-4457

Australia 08 8277 1555
Canada 1-800-465-7301
Europe .... +44 (0) 113 278 1708
New Zealand 09-309-1890

HUMAN KINETICS
The Premier Publisher for Sports & Fitness
P.O. Box 5076 • Champaign, IL 61825-5076 USA